Praise for
Lioness Arising

"*Lioness Arising* will cause you to see the awesome strength and beauty that God has given every woman. It will stir up the lioness heart in you and inspire you to rise above the daily grind of life and serve God with a renewed passion."

—JOYCE MEYER, best-selling author and Bible teacher

"Lisa Bevere not only inspires us with roaring truths but also lives the life of a lioness. She is a committed Christian, a strong wife, a fearless mother, a bold speaker, and an extraordinary writer. *Lioness Arising* will inspire you to fulfill your God-purposed role in establishing God's kingdom on earth. It is one of the most stirring books we have ever read."

—JAMES and BETTY ROBISON, *Life Today* television

"*Lioness Arising* will help you to awaken the seeds of greatness God has placed inside you. Lisa's passion to empower others will help you discover your value, purpose, and the amazing gifts you have to offer the world around you."

—VICTORIA OSTEEN, co-pastor, Lakewood Church, Houston, TX

"Lisa Bevere sends out a clarion call to women everywhere to rise up and take hold of the power God has given them. Whatever stage of life you are in, *Lioness Arising* will empower you to realize the strength, courage, and direction God has set before you."

—ED YOUNG, pastor, Fellowship Church, and author of *You!
The Journey to the Center of Your Worth*

"As a co-laborer for the cause of Christ, Lisa Bevere reminds us that the feminine form embodies love, hope, joy, and tenderness, without sacrificing courage, strength, and confidence. This book will remind you that God sees our dreams before we ever see them ourselves. It will inspire you to rise up in your calling and advance Christ's kingdom across the earth."

—BRIAN and BOBBIE HOUSTON, senior pastors, Hillsong Church, Australia

"Compelling and thought-provoking, *Lioness Arising* will challenge you to be all God designed you to be."

> —MARGARET FEINBERG, author of *The Sacred Echo*
> and *Scouting the Divine*

"Lisa Bevere's prayer is that something fierce, beautiful, and wild will be awakened in you as you read this book. *Lioness Arising* will live up to its title because Lisa is someone who makes the world a better place."

> —DINO RIZZO, lead pastor, Healing Place Church

"Hope will arise as you catch a glimpse of what could happen if every woman was fully awake in her moment in history. Read this book and awaken the lioness in you!"

> —CHARLOTTE GAMBILL, founder and director, Cherish Women's Ministries, and senior associate pastor, Abundant Life Church, UK

"*Lioness Arising* shows Lisa Bevere's God-given ability to shed light on spir-itual principles as she shapes a world where women rise up as the fierce and beautiful lionesses they were created to be."

> —CHRISTINE CAINE, director, Equip & Empower Ministries, and founder, The A21 Campaign

"In her own honest and compelling way, Lisa challenges us to rise courageously. I felt empowered, hopeful, and encouraged to take my place as a lioness among many others."

> —HOLLY WAGNER, author of *God Chicks*

"A timely message for women in the Body of Christ, Lisa gives a clear directive for the lioness to arise and take her place in defense of the faith."

> —JENTEZEN FRANKLIN, senior pastor, Free Chapel and *New York Times* best-selling author of *Fasting*

LIONESS ARISING

Wake Up and Change Your World

LISA BEVERE

WATERBROOK
PRESS

LIONESS ARISING
PUBLISHED BY WATERBROOK PRESS
12265 Oracle Boulevard, Suite 200
Colorado Springs, Colorado 80921

ISBN 978-0-307-45779-0
ISBN 978-0-307-45780-6 (electronic)

The Library of Congress has cataloged the hardcover edition as follows:
Bevere, Lisa.
    Lioness arising : wake up and change your world / Lisa Bevere. — 1st ed.
        p. cm.
    Includes bibliographical references (p.   ).
    ISBN 978-0-307-45778-3 — ISBN 978-0-307-45780-6 (electronic)
    1. Christian women—Religious life. 2. Lion—Behavior—Miscellanea. I. Title.
    BV4527.B4945 2010
    248.8'43—dc22

                                        2010021331

Printed in the United States of America
2011—First Trade Paperback Edition

10 9 8 7 6 5 4 3 2 1

To all my lioness sisters

who feel something wild, fierce,

and beautiful stirring within them.

You are stunning.

You were born for this moment.

Don't be afraid of your strength, questions, or insights.

Awaken, rise up, and dare to realize

all you were created to be.

Contents

Awaken a Lioness

Nature is made to conspire with spirit to emancipate us.

RALPH WALDO EMERSON

The year was 1994, and it was a night like any other in that season of my life. I had tumbled into bed later than I should have after a desperate attempt at putting my house in order. As a pregnant mother of three sons, I slept deeply in those days. I would shut my eyes and fall right to sleep, only to be roused by the sound of an alarm, children, or late-morning sunlight streaming into my room. But this night I fell asleep and woke at dawn, shaken to my core.

In the predawn hours I'd experienced a vivid and unusual dream. Actually, to call it a dream makes it sound as though it came to me in the form of sleep or shadow; this imagery did not. I dream regularly, but not at this level of intensity. In my world of sleep, I found myself vibrantly awake. Before me was a scene set in another place and time. I sensed I no longer walked the pathways of earth. I stood in some heavenly realm, a place of illumination, without glare.

Radiant light was everywhere and appeared to come from everything. There was no mist or shadow, only glorious color. These saturated hues of living color were comprised of shades so concentrated that I am without earthly reference to name them. The pigments were layered and multi-dimensional. For some reason I best remember the tones of purple (but not quite our purple) and blue (yet unlike ours). There were no edges, sides, or upper border, yet the backdrop of color enwrapped what it showcased—an elevated platform of flawless, cream-colored stone, and on this platform reclined a golden lioness.

She was feline perfection—majestic, powerful, and richly textured. She didn't move, but there was no doubt in my mind that she was alive—far more alive than any earthbound animal I'd seen in motion. Her head was erect but not tense, and her forelegs stretched out in front of her. Her fur and eyes gleamed golden. Beneath her flawless, tawny coat, I could see every curve of her perfectly formed muscles. This stunning, still lioness was far more substantial, vivid, and vibrant than any of the lionesses that now walk our earth. I couldn't help thinking I beheld a heavenly prototype.

Etched on the front of the flawless pillar platform were both a word and a roman numeral: Numbers XXIII.

In contrast with this lioness, my form felt transparent, insignificant, and strangely out of place. I felt detached from my body and unaware of being pregnant. I knew I was there *to behold and see,* to keenly observe—and in doing so, to learn something unrealized. I sensed an urgency to grasp the weight of the imagery. Even though I was alone with a lioness, I felt no alarm or threat. I felt only wide-eyed wonder, as though by seeing, my spirit was being enlarged and connected. I absorbed all I could of what was around me. My focus shifted, and I looked into the eyes of the lioness. As I did, I heard a voice somewhere behind me announce: *With the birth of this son, you will awaken a lioness.*

In a blur of golden light, majesty, and wonder, it was over. The next thing I knew, it was morning, and I was fully awake. All my senses were in a state of high alert, not out of fear as much as out of shock. What had I just witnessed? As time has passed, I have come to believe our earth is the time-tethered, shadowed form or partial revelation of what is original, timeless, and whole in heaven.

RISE UP LIKE A LIONESS

As I lay in the gray of dawn, wide awake, heart racing, and body trembling, I sensed God had sent me this vision of a lioness to reveal something I would have easily missed in the day-to-day. He had my full attention. I was listening with every sense engaged. My room seemed faded and hollow, a stark contrast to the world of color I'd just left. The morning sounds of earth were muffled compared to the clarion voice in the otherworldly place. I paused, afraid to move and lose the last remnants of the vision. I closed my eyes. Yes, it was all there—the lioness, the platform, the inscription, the backdrop, and the voice.

Time passed, my heart slowed, my body calmed, and I opened my eyes. Curious about the inscription on the front of the platform, I reached out and drew my Bible into bed with me. I wondered, was there a connection with a literal chapter or verse? If so, what did Numbers 23 hold? As I flipped through the pages, my heart sank when I noted the translator's heading and discovered the passage was an oracle of Balaam. I knew he was an accurate, but dishonorable, prophet. I read on, not sensing much of anything until I came to verse 19.

> God is not a man, so he does not lie.
>> He is not human, so he does not change his mind.
> Has he ever spoken and failed to act?
>> Has he ever promised and not carried it through?
> Listen, I received a command to bless;
>> God has blessed, and I cannot reverse it!
> No misfortune is in his plan for Jacob;
>> no trouble is in store for Israel.
> For the LORD their God is with them;
>> he has been proclaimed their king.
> God brought them out of Egypt;
>> for them he is as strong as a wild ox.
> No curse can touch Jacob;
>> no magic has any power against Israel.
> For now it will be said of Jacob,
>> "What wonders God has done for Israel!" (Numbers 23:19–23, NLT)

These words contain so much about the faithfulness of God. His promises are sure and certain, and his blessings are irreversible. Because of God's faithfulness, Israel had a future secure and free from the tainted and twisted effects of witchcraft or curses. All this was reassuring, but the next verse was riveting.

These people rise up like a lioness,
*   like a majestic lion rousing itself.*
They refuse to rest
    until they have feasted on prey,
        drinking the blood of the slaughtered! (Numbers 23:24, NLT)

Trembling, I reread the fierce words printed on the fragile page: *rise up like a lioness, like a majestic lion rousing itself.* The raw imagery hit me. I could see it: a lion and his lioness, rising up out of the grass. As they rose, the dynamics of the plain changed from peaceful to electric. Every living creature sensed the lions' change of posture and watched attentively. The golden ones were awake, stretching, testing the air, surveying their domain, ready to make their move. Perhaps they were hungry. Maybe they were agitated by the presence of an enemy who had violated the marked boundaries of their territory, and it was time to make their presence known.

Once they were up, tensions would be high until their movements ceased. If the lions were restless, there'd be no rest for the other creatures until the lions had fought or feasted, then resettled.

With their rising, I sensed a stirring of their strength in my spirit as well. Who isn't awed and captivated when a lion or lioness rises and moves out from its resting place? It is a wonder to behold. But what was this to me? How could I possibly be connected to any of this wild, golden might?

While the imagery thrilled me, it also repelled me. I liked the idea of lionesses napping in the sun as their young frolicked, but images of the hunt and kill frightened and even disgusted me. When I watched *National Geographic* or *Wild Kingdom,* I averted my eyes as the big cats took down impalas and zebras.

5

As these thoughts flashed through my mind, I recalled the words of the night vision: "With the birth of this son, you will awaken a lioness." What could this mean? I saw no connection between the powerful, fearless lioness and the large, pregnant woman who lay in my bed. To say I was a lioness was laughable. I was a tofu-eating, borderline vegan, not a bloodthirsty predator. I was terrified by almost everything outside my control and intimidated by the majority of the people I met. I found strong, dominant women especially frightening.

My pregnancy had been somewhat of a reprieve. In an impassioned moment of prayer a few months before my son's conception, I'd laid aside all my protests and told God, "Okay, okay! I'm yours. Have your way in my life! I'll do anything you want. I'll even talk to women if you want me to." Though at the time I had no idea what I might say.

When I became pregnant, I figured all bets were off. I imagined the commission and my compliance had been a test of sorts—like Abraham's willingness to sacrifice his son Isaac. Perhaps I'd get bonus points for being willing and I'd never have to follow through on my pledge.

But with this vision, it appeared my pre-pregnancy deal still stood.

And what was this about a son?

Throughout my pregnancy I'd assumed I was carrying a daughter. Everyone I came in contact with told me I was having a girl. No one had mentioned the possibility of a boy. I was the only one who harbored the secret hope for another son.

I shook my head in disbelief. *If* any of this was true and I was about to morph into a lioness of sorts, then surely someone else would see this impending transformation as well. This vision was going to require some serious secondary confirmation.

LOOKING FOR AFFIRMATION

A few weeks passed, and a woman evangelist I had immense respect for came into town. Here was my chance! She'd invited another pregnant friend and me to join her for lunch. My friend was an exceptional businesswoman who'd experienced a radical conversion and was shaking her region of Asia with the gospel. *Perhaps the lioness vision was for her…* I decided to casually bring up the idea over lunch and watch her reaction.

Our lunch date fell on a gorgeous, sunny day in Winter Park, Florida. After the three of us roamed the streets for a while, I finally plopped my pregnant self down for lunch and wondered how I could introduce the lioness into our girlfriend-shopping conversation. Later as we ate, my opening came.

My friend told us she was expecting a girl, and the evangelist said she was excited about the prospect of me having a daughter as well.

"But what if it's another boy?" I asked.

She was aghast that I would even raise such a possibility. After all, she reasoned, I had three sons, and John needed a girl to dote on. Right then I decided to relay the story of the lioness and the proclamation of a son.

I'm not certain what I said made sense. Actually, I know it didn't. After all, I was far from convinced myself. I knew the vision was real, but in my nervousness I still discounted my connection with the lioness imagery. I kept talking, trying to process my encounter, but how could I expect them to understand when I was confused? My ramblings reflected on their concerned faces. Realizing I had hit an impasse, I stopped abruptly.

There was a long pause in the awkward aftermath as the minister looked doubtfully at me and then asked, "When is your baby due?"

"October tenth," I answered sheepishly, relieved to say something that made sense.

Leaning back, she shook her head and said with confidence, "No, no, you could not *possibly* be a lioness by then."

I wanted to yell, "I agree!" but feeling slightly ridiculous, I merely nodded. On one level I felt relief and on the other slightly annoyed, definitely embarrassed, and possibly insulted.

What did she mean I couldn't be a lioness by then? It was only springtime, and October was more than five months away! After all, how long could this lioness transformation take? Why had I shared my vision anyway? I should have waited until I found out if I was carrying a son.

She sensed my confusion and explained, "There is still too much stuff in you that God needs to work out... You will not be free by October."

Well, there you go. Even though I didn't like the woman's bluntness, I agreed with her assessment. Slowly the conversation returned to its previously normal rhythm as I closed my mouth and allowed my thoughts to turn inward. She had only voiced what she saw obviously reflected in me. I was plagued by doubt and insecurity on many levels. Even my husband, John, was constantly saying to me, "It must be so hard to live in your mind, Lisa, with so many worries and fears crowding in on you." He was right. And it was getting harder and harder all the time. I was tired of being a long-term restoration project.

No More Excuses

For years I'd been making excuses for myself. I was a cancer survivor and a stay-at-home mom with a dysfunctional past, who just wanted to survive her preschool children. Was it possible that God thought I was destined for more? Was something powerful and slightly fierce waiting to be awakened inside me? Maybe I'd wear courage well. After all, hadn't I been adventurous when I was young? There was a time when my dream job ideas ranged between assassin and astronaut.

Yes, I wanted to recover some of the strength I'd forfeited while trying to fit in as a pastor's wife and a nice Christian woman. I was ready to stretch a bit and rise up in strength and beauty. I was tired of being thought of as weak and whiny. I was tired of revisiting the pain of my past. I was up for a challenge. I loved that my husband was passionate and strong, but I was tired of hiding behind him. Tired of wearying my mind with so many things that didn't matter. Tired of pretending. Maybe the vision of a lioness was just what I needed! Rather than nice and safe, I was ready to be seen as slightly fierce and definitely focused.

I drove home after lunch that day, gripping the steering wheel more tightly than necessary. I was willing to try on this lioness vibe in the relative safety of my Honda Civic. I rolled down the windows and bounced to the latest in contemporary Christian music, and I let the wind rather than the air conditioning shake my "mane." It all seems a bit silly now (especially since lionesses don't have manes). Through my cat-shaped Ray-Ban lenses, I saw my frizzy, highlighted hair in the side-view mirror… *Wait, do I see wild lioness gold in those tresses?*

Not ready by October? Ha! I'll show you! I'm a lioness!

Somehow through the combination of my lunch faux pas, my friend's blunt assessment, and a series of other unrelated events, an interesting transformation began to take shape. It was as though a gauntlet had been thrown down and a challenge had been issued.

With the birth of my son Arden Christopher (his name means "fiery, determined, anointed one"), something within me shifted. Even though another child meant more of a mother load, I became a focused daughter. You see, like many other mothers, my God-connected self had been strained. I was almost at the point of drowning in my day-to-day life. I was so caught up with my ever-expanding and increasingly demanding to-do list, I'd forgotten who I was. I was full of self-doubt. My life was small, self-centered, isolated, petty, safe, and ineffective. I remembered my name, whom I was married to, and who my kids were, but what I did and who I was responsible for overshadowed my sense of being God's daughter.

As I paused, God began to whisper strength to me and to call me by another name. To everyone else I had a name that was attached to a job description. I was mother to my children, wife to my husband, pastor's wife to the congregation, but to God Most High I was simply *daughter*. As I focused on just being his and what all that meant, life and strength flowed into my days, and rest entered my soul. My heart enlarged.

After Arden's birth, I began to step out of the shadow of my insecurities, fears, comfort zone, and failures and began to reach out to others. I wrote my first book, *Out of Control and Loving It!*, while nursing Arden. Writing this book opened up another world to me. Suddenly I was out speaking to women across our nation who were hungry for authenticity. In response to their hurt and hunger and the glaring need for healthy female connections, I wrote more books.

Time passed, we moved from our home in sunny, hot, and humid Florida to another home in sunny, cold, and dry Colorado. The move to Colorado drew our family indoors and around the table more. It also positioned us to weather many transitions. A few times over the next decade (almost too few to note), I was singled out or called a lioness. I would just smile, content that

I was no longer a frightened, timid, domestic cat. I imagined the lioness story was over and my personal transformation almost complete.

But I was wrong.

IT'S NOT ABOUT YOU, LISA

In the fall of 2007, the lioness visited me again. I was one of many women ministering at a women's conference in the stunning land of New Zealand. This event was so well attended that the host church had to do two back-to-back conferences to accommodate all the women.

The first conference was held at the church, and the second was held in an Auckland arena. We had finished conference number one and were at the arena for conference number two. The sessions had begun. The ministers were able, compassionate, faithful stewards of the Word. But for some unknown reason, I felt troubled during the afternoon break. It wasn't that I felt pressured to prepare—I would be duplicating what I had said in the first conference. Still, I felt an urgency to pray before my session. It was as though there was some sort of resistance. I knew it was not from the attendees, who had chosen to be there, nor from any of the speakers or the host church. We were all of one heart and had come ready to worship, preach, and encourage the women. But there was something else in the mix. Perhaps God was trying to get my attention. I had to get alone and sort my way through it, so I headed off to my hotel room, which overlooked the Auckland harbor.

I paced my room, stretching my arms out toward the harbor, praying for God's direction and insight and singing along with the music on my iPod, "Shout unto God with a voice of triumph." To position my heart, I began to thank God for various things he was doing in my life. I had just completed the final edits on my *Nurture* manuscript and began to thank God that the writing and editing process was over. For me, writing a book is like going through labor, so my prayer went something like, *Thank you, God. It is finished!* I exalted, *I don't want to write again anytime soon!*

Suddenly I sensed God speak to my spirit. *I am sorry you feel that way…because I need you to write again.*

What? God *needed* me?

He went on. *I am releasing strategies from heaven. They will be found in my Word. You will not have all of these strategies by any means, but you will have a measure of them. You must write and record what I speak to you so that when my daughters gather, there will be a whole picture. If you do not bring your piece of the puzzle, the picture will not be complete.*

Suddenly the lioness was again before me.

As I beheld her in all her strength and fierce beauty, I heard the Voice say, *I said with the birth of your son, you would* awaken a lioness. *I did not say you were the lioness.*

Immediately I saw how limited, silly, and human my perspective had been. The Voice went on to say, *Jesus is the Lion of the tribe of Judah, and it is time his bride awakens a lioness. Study the ways and aspects of the lioness.*

Then I heard the first strategy:

Lionesses hunt together.

I was taken aback. Was what I was hearing even scriptural? What could all this mean? Women were beginning to get used to the idea that there is power in femininity and value in their capacity to nurture. Now God was telling me to call them lionesses? How did this fit in?

I wondered, *Could it be God wants to awaken something fierce and wild within his women?*

Numbers 23 came before me once again, and I saw in it a charge for Christian women to rise up. Right then and there I set my heart to study the lioness and to search out the parallels for God's daughters. I've spent the last two years researching, observing, and writing about lionesses. Initially I thought of making connections between women and lionesses only on a literary level—without sharing the vision God gave me—but as time passed, I realized this vision was not meant to remain mine alone. I was not shown the lioness because I am favored or special. Nor did I experience this imagery because I am highly visionary. I was shown this because God knew one day I'd be someone with a voice.

Time and time again as I have spoken the phrase "you will awaken a lioness," I have literally seen it impact women. Sometimes they respond with quiet tears as something within them is watered. At other times they gasp as though they've breathed in the revelation and realized it is okay to be beautiful and fierce. I believe the response has been so overwhelmingly positive because, just as there is a lamb of sorts hidden within, there is also a lioness within every one of God's daughters. And it is time she awakens.

When I think of a lioness, a smile plays along my mouth. I throw back my shoulders and stand a bit straighter. More than any other creature, the lioness makes me proud to be a female. There is no doubting her strength. I also imagine there is no creature that makes a man prouder to be a male than the lion. The lion is the king of the jungle, and there is no question about who is the queen.

LOOK...AND LEARN

This isn't the first time God has pointed us back to the simplicity of creation to restore our perspective. Jesus admonishes us to consider the flowers and to learn from them that God will clothe and care for us (see Matthew 6:28;

Luke 12:27). Likewise, the heavenly realms declare God's glory and make an open show of his righteousness (see Psalm 19:1; Psalm 50:6).

> The heavens declare His righteousness,
>> And all the peoples see His glory. (Psalm 97:6, NKJV)

The wild, fierce beauty of creation is but a window that offers a glimpse of the God who created us. We need to throw open this window and allow God's untamed, limitless beauty to awaken a heavenly awe within us. As we open our eyes to the wonder of creation, it arouses a God-yearning. Our spirit will respond to what it sees. Creation declares, "There is more! More than what you see. More than what you hear. More than mere human mortality. There is the Immortal God who is seated on high."

Jesus our Christ came as the Lamb slain before the foundations of the earth, but the book of Revelation also reveals him as a Lion:

> But one of the twenty-four elders said to me, "Stop weeping! Look, *the Lion of the tribe of Judah,* the heir to David's throne, has won the victory. He is worthy to open the scroll and its seven seals." (Revelation 5:5, NLT)

He is *both* our Lion and our Lamb. I wonder, could there be a combination of two more contrasting images? The Message version says this lion of Judah "can rip through the seven seals." John, the author of Revelation, wept because after a search of all of heaven, earth, and even the underworld, not one was found worthy to tear open the seven seals and begin the progressive reveal. Then the elder nearest John encouraged him to *look,* for there was a revelation of a Lion in our Lamb. He alone is worthy and initiates this work of unsealing.

A rip or tear is a violent release. I am immediately reminded of the thick curtain of separation in the temple as it was ripped or rent in two (see Mark 15:38). The tear began at the highest place and ended at the lowest. I love this, for our God is always tearing asunder that which would hinder or separate any of us from all of him. In the divinely mysterious book of Revelation, this act of unsealing the scrolls of heaven sets things in motion on earth.

> **Nature is made to conspire with spirit to emancipate us.**
>
> —RALPH WALDO EMERSON

Even now I sense God longing to unseal and reveal a portion of himself to and in every one of us. If not, why would he have written this dramatic end of our earth story if it did not contain a revelation for each of us? I believe we are invited again not to despair or to weep but to lift up our eyes, look, and truly see.

Our earth echoes the revelations and wisdom of heaven.

How amazing that our heavenly Father designed his creation to open our hearts. Each plant, animal, element, and landscape says, "Arise and be all you were created to be." According to Job, nature has the potential to teach us.

> God sets out the entire creation as a science classroom,
>   using birds and beasts to teach wisdom. (Job 35:11)

The wonder of God's love and the extent to which he will go to impart his wisdom to us is almost too vast to grasp. But we should not be surprised by this. He is, after all, the Creator, who declares:

Every creature in the forest is mine,
  the wild animals on all the mountains.
I know every mountain bird by name;
  the scampering field mice are my friends.
If I get hungry, do you think I'd tell you?
  All creation and its bounty are mine. (Psalm 50:10–12)

We isolate ourselves from the creatures of the earth, but God knows them by name. Do we imagine that he cares nothing for his creation? He fashioned creation for himself. Nature has much to reveal about its Creator, if we will but listen to it. In Proverbs we are charged, "You lazy fool, look at an ant. Watch it closely; let it teach you a thing or two" (6:6).

I believe God is asking us to do something similar now. He is asking us to look at the lioness and to learn. He invites us: *Daughters, look at the lioness. Watch her closely. Let her awaken your untamed nature, your fierce beauty, and your unbridled strength so you can rise up and be the courageous women I have called you to be.*

How does a lioness reveal strength and courage in women? And how can women rise up like the lioness? Each of us will have our unique response, but this glimpse of lioness characteristics may give you insight. In the following chapters, we'll look at several reasons a lioness arises from her leisurely repose in the African sun:

She rises to gather strength.

She rises to greet and groom others.

She rises to hunt.

She rises alongside other lionesses.

She rises to move the young to safety.

She rises to confront enemies that threaten the pride.

She rises to walk with her king.

I have come to see the lioness as a picture of how every daughter of the Most High can embrace her strength, develop courage, and effect change in her world. Is there a lioness hidden within you? It is my prayer that by the time you finish this book, you'll have your answer, and with that answer something fierce, beautiful, and wild will be awakened in you.

2

A Force Unseen

> If ever there comes a time when the women
> of the world come together purely and simply
> for the benefit of mankind, it will be a force
> such as the world has never known.
>
> MATTHEW ARNOLD, NINETEENTH-CENTURY
> BRITISH POET AND PHILOSOPHER

Could it be we've awakened in this moment? I've had the privilege of witnessing the foreshadowing of this gathered force. In the faraway land down under, in Europe, and even in my homeland of the United States, I have seen the first fruits of what will no doubt prove to be a full-fledged movement. From the quickening of a daughter, the gathering is quickly growing into a woman. Did the words of this poet and philosopher speak to something unrealized deep within you? When I first read this quote, I was arrested and literally felt my breath catch.

19

I can only imagine *my* physical response was a reaction to the enormity of *our* unrealized possibilities. You already know from the title of this book that I long to awaken something wild, wise, and wonderful in you. I challenge you to ponder this idea of women coming together for good. Reread the quote if necessary, because the hope within it is indeed worthy of more than a glance; this insight deserves your full attention.

Dare to ask yourself, could Matthew Arnold's words be more than theory, political rhetoric, or hopeful conjecture? Could his insight be providential, permissive, or even prophetic? Did he look ahead and see the daughters of our time and encourage us to gather now from his distant perspective of then? Did he know this gathering would not, could not, happen in his day yet hope this assembly would happen in ours? Did he realize how great the need of our time would become? Did he notice you and me in this moment?

I believe the truest answers to these questions lie deep within each woman and are best played out, not with words, but by how she chooses to live. Our potential to play a part in this answer of women will be known by how we respond to our space in time. Our choices will be further revealed in how we choose to position both our sons and daughters so they likewise will choose well.

> The solution to adult problems tomorrow depends on large measure upon how our children grow up today.
>
> —Margaret Mead

Will the women of our time yet rise above the many conflicting and limiting worldwide cultural and religious images and the resulting prejudices against women? Will our brave sisters overseas move forward even with the absence of encouragement from many sectors? Will we in the Western world turn from frivolous distractions and focus our attention on worthy and noble causes?

Will we supersede the conflicting noise and arguments that say our contribution is not necessary, not God breathed? Will we apprehend the gravity and urgency of our time and lay aside our doctrinal differences and opinions in order to join ranks? Will the age gap close as we join hearts and hands? Will we come to the unity of faith? Will this unified faith merely express itself as a set of beliefs?

Will this unity be forced or vibrant? Could this shared faith be quickened through works and reveal us as stewards of something at once evident, irresistible, fierce, and substantial?

Will our coming together openly illustrate all we dare hope for and be a living declaration of all we truly believe? Could this faith extend itself by selflessly reaching out and giving rather than turning in and taking? I pray so, because only then will we find our world enlarged and the lives of others impacted by our stretch.

Yes, I understand that all I ask and hope for is a bit of a stretch right now, but we will reach no further without such a stretch. It is not enough to look solely at where we are. If we are to spread out, we must look back, around, and ahead.

By looking back to the eighteen hundreds, we see a time when women had little or no voice. By looking around, we realize the importance of our voice. By looking ahead, we know we must construct our words and lives in such a manner that we build wisely in the future.

It is time to enlarge the way we see and interact with so many areas of life. This dynamic of stretch happens when tension, flex, or strain is added to a muscle group. An ability to stretch can produce increased flexibility and prevent injury.

It is my hope to add some stretch to your life by introducing the lioness. I want her to expand how you view yourself, your femininity, your beauty, your strength, your purpose, your marriage, your world, and your God. Allow the lioness to challenge your interactions and develop your relationships with men, friends, and family. Even the lioness knows she must stretch before she attempts a pounce.

Before us lies the tension of both our personal life and the needs of the world. To cover this vast realm, we will need a vision that encompasses both.

AT EASE WITH STRENGTH, AT REST WITH POWER

Before we go any further, I want to discuss a question that arose after the vision. I wondered, *Why a lioness at ease above a scripture depicting God's people engaged in such consuming violence?* As time has passed, I have pondered the vision and all the thoughts the revelation has awakened (and yet awakens) within me. Here are some things I have gleaned.

God did not show me a lioness and then expect me to respond to her with passivity or fear. Her imagery exposed and contradicted my limited, fearful vantage. This lioness was an instrument that opened my eyes to a wider vista and enlarged my range of motion.

As I have traveled, I have seen some magnificent statues. Denmark, Rome, London, and Paris have monuments that pay tribute to awesome feats of strength and celebrate past conquests and moments of historic liberation. I have photographed these works of art and marveled at how their elegance and timeless beauty yet speak.

But the lioness of my vision was not a statue—she was a revelation.

Revelations carry elements of exposure and surprise. The lioness certainly surprised and exposed me as I stood before her pregnant and trembling in my pajamas. Though she never moved, she was more alive than I. In the light of her beauty and strength, I realized what I had lost. Because of fear, I had forfeited strength, life, and beauty. I had lost a sense of my true self, and with that loss so much of what God wanted for me was yet unrealized.

I am reminded of how the Israelites saw themselves as grasshoppers and the inhabitants of Canaan as giants, but we know from Numbers 23 that the inhabitants saw the Israelites as a lion and a lioness arising.

This contrast between perspective and reality comes into play when we compare our lioness sister with ourselves. Could we ever be like her? Will we ever be women who are at ease with our strength and at rest with our power? Will we wear our beauty comfortably?

The lioness imagery of might pared with respite is one we should embrace.

When the time came, the lioness roused herself. It is time you knew who you are. It is time you stirred, provoked, incited, and awakened yourself.

I have discovered this dynamic of *ease with strength and rest with power* is a very telling and beautiful image of a godly woman. Lovely ones, I give you permission to be at ease with your strength and at rest with your power.

Usually these pairings of *ease with strength and rest with power* come with the passage of time. They fuse as you begin to realize there is a power that abides within. Just as righteousness is a state we rest in, there is a realm where strength is a haven as well. We discover rest when we cease from striving.

> Your salvation requires you to turn back to me
> and stop your silly efforts to save yourselves.
> *Your strength will come from settling down*
> *in complete dependence on me*— (Isaiah 30:15)

There we have it! I can't imagine a better way to put it. Settle down, depend on him, and your strength will come. When we stop struggling in our own ability, our true strength is revealed. God is not withholding strength from you; he's bestowing it.

In contrast to our friend the lioness, I've seen many women terrified by their own strength. They recoil in fear if ideas, questions, or passions arise unbidden within them. Strength is not to be feared; it is to be embraced. Do not make the mistake of imagining meekness to be weakness. It is tempered strength or might under control.

Moses was called both meek and humble, but he was nevertheless a mighty leader and a force to be reckoned with. I have to wonder if this was because he had met the very One who was backing his every word.

An isolated awareness of good and evil overwhelms our human nakedness and begs a divine answer. Walking the realm of good outside of God limits us. Our present world issues are so incredibly vast they need limitless answers.

Like Moses we need a revelation of God's goodness to calm our trembling earth.

So, lovely one, will you dare to believe that you might be a part of this revelation of good and therefore gather with others and strategize so God's goodness will be seen through us?

Virtuous and Capable

I have intentionally not limited this "good" to the realm of "nice" or even "safe." It is a force, after all. I have likewise heard *virtue* described as a force.

> Who can find a virtuous and capable wife?
>   She is more precious than rubies.
>   Her husband can trust her,
>   and she will greatly enrich his life. (Proverbs 31:10–11, NLT)

Single women, before you imagine this verse leaves you out, remember Jesus is your bridegroom. It is not a question of who is included; we all are.

The question that arises is, can we be trusted with this charge? Will we enrich the lives of those around us? Will we be at once both capable and virtuous? Or will he find us divided into segments: some who are virtuous and others who are capable? The expression of one but not the other is not enough. We need an honorable gathering of virtuous women who are well able. What will we need to be capable of? Quite simply, anything and everything. We will need to be daughters capable of whatever is necessary.

Over the last decade I've met many amazing women who encourage others to realize what they are capable of. Because of the increased awareness of need, women are intentionally focusing their educational pursuits and developing specific areas of talents so they will have a capable response.

They are bright enough to respectively pose questions from an enlightened vantage of insight and relevancy. They've learned to add in necessary qualities so they can grow into all they truly are. These women are talented and gifted, fearless yet honoring, connected yet self-contained, present yet far reaching, compassionate yet fierce, pure but not naive, strong and gentle, simple yet highly strategic.

> It is not enough to outline gigantic programs on paper. I must write my ideas on the earth.
>
> —EMILE PEREIRE

If our plans and programs do not translate and affect the earth and its inhabitants, then they are only theory. Programs need to come alive. They only work if we can lend voice, hands, and feet to them.

Our world has known the impact of many forces. Over the centuries our earth has been bludgeoned by forces of nature such as hurricanes, tsunamis, and monsoons. The earth's shell has been split and its foundations shaken by earthquakes. Armed forces have gathered for motives and purposes both noble and foul. Coalitions of armed forces have met on battlefields and left destruction in their wake.

But what of a force that did not revel in its power to intimidate, threaten, or destroy? Members of this force would have strategic and unique roles—some seen, others unseen, but all valued. What if this force was at once selfless in motive and simplistic in its objective? What might it look and sound like?

Alexander the Great said,

I am not afraid of an army of lions led by a sheep; I am afraid of an army of sheep led by a lion.

What an amazing picture of us. We are an army of sheep led by a Lion. Since we follow a Lion, we should not war like timid sheep. We are meek in the way we follow and fierce in the way we fight. In this manner, gentle and fierce meet and are comfortable. If we study the natural course and history of human forces, we witness a pattern; there is a rise to power, a corruption of strength, a loss of power, and a collapse from within.

But what if there is another model? What if there is an unformed and yet unexpressed force?

I type this book in a much larger font than it will be printed in, because it is getting harder for me to see the small and up close. Yet my vision for the large and far away has increased immeasurably.

In the distance I see two conflicting images: great trouble and magnificent victory. On shores near and far, I see deep, dark oppression, but I also see a glorious uprising. I see gross wickedness and global injustice exposed and conquered on many fronts by an encounter with God's inescapable light and his unassailable justice. I see his daughters stretching forth like lionesses preparing to pounce. I see all this in our future. No doubt nothing I've said surprises you. Like you, I do not see these things because I read the paper. I see them because I have eyes to see in the Spirit.

But I not only see…I hear. I have heard cries in the distance and cries up close. I have listened to the plight of hopeless ones trapped in prisons of darkness. Each day is a struggle against the stifling oppression, which threatens to silence their voices and then reach beyond to muffle the cries of their children. These desperate mothers' only hope is for something more for their children. One young mother begged us to take her eight-year-old daughter, because the young child hid under the bed as she serviced clients. Thankfully, Life Outreach, a ministry of James and Betty Robison, rescued this daughter, but the mother, who was afraid to leave, remains behind in the brothel—overwhelmed by despair.

WIND WORDS

There are times I am overwhelmed by what I hear as well.

Why?

It is easier *not* to have seen or heard. Because this is true, most turn from these disturbing sounds and images and quickly fill their ears and eyes with distractions. It is the very reason tourism thrives alongside sex trafficking. I watched as foreign visitors to Thailand pretended that what they saw was perhaps a perpetual party. One U.S. businessman I spoke with acted as though his lewdness was boosting the Thai economy.

Anyone with ears to hear should listen and understand! (Matthew 11:15, NLT)

This charge did not stop when Jesus, the Son of Man, ascended and took his rightful place as the Son of God. In the book of Revelation, he again expounds on the urgency and desperate need for a people who are brave enough to listen.

> Are your ears awake? Listen. Listen to the Wind Words, the Spirit blowing through the churches. (Revelation 2:7)

We must answer his question. Are our ears awake?

Better yet, do we want our ears awakened? Lovely ones, we are all in the process of not only hearing but truly listening. As I wake, I nudge you to ask, "Did you hear that sound?"

Sadly, I fear we are like a sleepy bride who tosses and turns on her luxurious bed, surrounded by pillows in an attempt to muffle the very sound that might awaken her. How loud must the alarm of our time become before we are aroused and fully awake?

In addition to the obvious screech of our hurting world, there is another sound calling to us. But it does not scream. With all the noise it is the sound you must strain to hear. It is the still, small voice of the Spirit. This sound rises in volume as we each choose to respond.

I love the terminology "Wind Words." God has set his word upon the winds. The Holy Spirit is likened to a wind, or stream of air, carrying words that whisper life and power. We cannot see the wind, but we see its effect. Wind has the power to blow things into your world and to blow things away. Its energy propels ships or silently strands them. The power of the wind whips up seas and erodes mountains. There are headwinds that fight forward progress and tailwinds that hurry us on our way. The wind repeatedly encircles our world, sometimes traveling quickly, other times slowly.

The wind carries the whisper of God from one place to another.

Often the interference of the artificial noise that surrounds us dulls our ability to attentively listen to the Spirit's *Wind Words*.

There is another hindrance to our ability to hear. It is the familiarity of having already heard. When we have heard something time and time again, we may tune it out and quit really listening.

If we think we know what somebody is going to say, we listen differently. A few years ago I found myself in just such a place as I read the Scriptures. I was so familiar with certain versions of the Bible that, as I read, I knew what was coming next. Perhaps you've had this happen. This caused me to lose some of my childlike wonder with God's Word. To counter my apathy, I began to delve into The Message paraphrase.

Why? I wanted to be surprised. For this reason I have quoted many of the passages from The Message so you too could experience a vantage of wonder. I am not replacing the Bible with a paraphrase. I'm just bringing in relevant language and additional research. But feel free to study your preferred Bible version as well.

I've done this because, like you, I truly want to hear. Once our ears are opened, we cannot help but lend the sound of our voices.

Speak up for those who cannot speak for themselves;
>   ensure justice for those being crushed.
Yes, speak up for the poor and helpless,
>   and see that they get justice. (Proverbs 31:8–9, NLT)

In this passage Solomon's mother, Bathsheba, is charging her son, the king, to lend his majestic voice to those who are crushed by the weight of injustice. It is also the setup or context for the verses on the virtuous woman (see Proverbs 31:10–31). Like Solomon's mother, will we encourage the men in our world to speak up for those who've had their voices silenced? We have been made kings and priests before our God. So even if others remain silent, we are to speak out.

As a "grand" mother, I want to know that what the sons and daughters inherit will be truly grand. More and more the consensus of global studies points to gender equality as the missing link to stem the tide of world poverty and even terrorism. In 2001 the World Bank produced an influential study, *Engendering Development: Through Gender Equality in Rights, Resources, and Voice,* arguing that promoting gender equality is crucial to combat global poverty. "'Investment in girls' education may well be the highest-return investment available in the developing world,' Lawrence Summers wrote when he was chief economist of the World Bank. 'The question is not whether countries can afford this investment, but whether countries can afford not to educate more girls.'"[1] The United Nations Development Programme also conducted a study that concluded, "Women's empowerment helps raise economic productivity."[2]

The terrorism of our time inspired security experts to conduct a gender study of their own, and this is what they found:

> The reason there are so many Muslim terrorists, they argued, has lit-
> tle to do with the Koran but a great deal to do with the lack of robust
> female participation in the economy and society of many Islamic
> countries.... Empowering girls, some in the military argued, would
> disempower terrorists.[3]

Great expense and effort went into these crucial, insightful, and exten-sive studies. I am always awed when our human wisdom points us back to what God has said all along. Long before there ever was a world problem, there was a world answer: woman.

> It is not good for the man to be alone. I will make a helper who is
> just right for him. (Genesis 2:18, NLT)

The man alone was not good. Now, just as then, adding women to life equations multiplies and brings goodness to men, women, children, and the world we all share together. An isolated life invites what is "not good." Humans were created for connections to one another. Even so, extensive alliances of only males appear to be a recipe for potential disaster. We can conclude from the insights of Genesis and current studies that dominant male-driven cultures are unhealthy on multiple levels.

You were not created to be subservient; you are a joint heir. Women are God-answers. The addition of women's voices increases the educational opportunity for all children, stimulates the economy, and apparently decreases the risk of terrorism.

But what does this answer of woman look like?

When I discovered and celebrated *my* feminine creation, I realized I was not an afterthought. As a daughter, wife, and mother, I was an answer. If I was an answer, then it was only logical that the sisters who surrounded my life were answers as well. We are not secondary citizens in the eyes of God. You, lovely one, have the potential to be a living, breathing solution to human problems.

As I travel and declare this simple truth over the lives of women young and old, I can barely explain their response. Women not only hear what I say with trembling hearts; they speak it out loud and believe.

"I am an answer."

In that moment there is a stretch, a revelation. Their eyes are reoriented and opened to see their feminine self the way God has always seen them…the one who completes.

Yet this realization is just our beginning.

Women are more than a collective economic stimulus. And with our ability to bring solutions, new questions will arise. We are writing a new bill of rights in which women are the friends of mankind. We gather to map out a world where women and children are welcomed, not exploited.

Here is some of what I know of heaven's daughter:

She is lovely, intelligent, and capable.

Her life is connected rather than isolated.

She is loved by God and hated by Satan.

She is oppressed worldwide by both subtle and obvious means.

The question remains: what might she be collectively if she was supported and strategic?

AWAKEN SOMETHING UNCONTAINABLE

I have had the privilege of traveling to Southeast Asia and India as a partner of Life Outreach in the hope of capturing stories compelling enough to release responses from others. I have witnessed the scourge of poverty and the outrage of sex trafficking as I traveled to Cambodia, Thailand, and Mumbai. I have also seen hope and the promise of restoration as people respond with generosity and as organizations begin to work together.

There is desperate need everywhere for cooperation and response. I was in the Ukraine, having breakfast with a friend, when a stunning young woman walked in. This is not unusual in a nation known for its beautiful women, but this one was in the company of a man who looked to be in his sixties. Dressed in high heels and hot pants, she couldn't have been more than eighteen. They were seated at a table right by us. I watched as the older man devoured his food while she sipped black coffee and stared blankly out the window. The young men behind the buffet table whispered, snickered, and pointed her way. It wasn't long before another man twice her age joined their table. I wanted to cry. The girl looked so lonely, so lost. It was obvious she was a high-priced call girl, but all we saw was a love-starved daughter playing dress-up, seated between two lecherous businessmen who were devouring her life.

I've spoken directly to some of our sisters who were trafficked. Yes, that is what they are—our sisters. They are not prostitutes by choice; they are victims and courageous survivors.

One long, humid day in India, I listened to story after story of heartbreak from a group of young girls and older women whom Life Outreach had gathered in a small apartment. They each told their story a bit differently—some with many tears, others without any apparent emotion.

I am sure they wondered why I wanted to hear their stories. Was I sympathetic? Did I judge them? Could I even understand? Would I have any answers?

One of these brave women, whom I will call Sama, reflected back to when she was a young girl from an outlying village in Nepal, filled with dreams and frustrated by her mother. One day an uncle overheard them arguing and pulled Sama aside. He offered to take her with him to Mumbai. There she'd find opportunity, education, and a chance to realize her dreams.

The promise was irresistible.

Before dawn, Sama and her uncle stole away from their small village. She braved a long and dangerous journey to slip out of Nepal into India.

Upon arriving in Mumbai, her uncle left her to rest in a shabby motel room. While she slept, her uncle sold her.

Sama woke confused and surrounded by strangers. It was time for her to work off the money her uncle had been paid.

Sama was taken to a local brothel and locked in a dark room. She had no idea what was about to happen. She didn't even speak the language. The door opened, and a client came in, expecting to be serviced. When she fought back, four women held her down while she was raped.

Sama was thirteen.

Time passed. Sama learned the language and worked off her debt, and in the process she became a canny businesswoman. With no other prospects and nowhere else to go, she rose within the brothel system to become a madam. She was the one who bought and sold the young girls. At her word the trafficked youths were held down. Sama oversaw the initiation of rape and ordered them beaten into submission.

When I met Sama, it was hard to believe any of this could be true. She was no longer a madam; she was a composed, middle-aged woman. Someone had shared God's love with her, and she had become a Christian. She had also been given an opportunity to get out. Sama found the courage to walk away from the brothels. She now works tirelessly to rescue the very girls she had once oppressed.

As we spoke, I tried to make sense of how Sama had ever become a madam. Had she forgotten what it was like to be that terrified thirteen-year-old girl? I asked her.

"Sama, how could you watch as young girls were kidnapped, raped, and beaten?"

She sighed as her head shook side to side.

"We did what we had to…to survive."

For many, survival is all they have.

I have climbed a mountain of refuse. I have walked filthy streets lined by houses so frail and makeshift that it's no wonder those who take shelter within their frames feel hopeless. I have slipped into brothels, disguised. I have seen the depressive lethargy of purposeless women in the West. I have watched as resources were wasted because we forgot who we were. I have seen the problems firsthand, and it is my desperate hope I will also see the answers.

Here is a stirring charge from the close of the inspiring and challenging book *Half the Sky*:

> The tide of history is turning women from beasts of burden and sexual playthings into full-fledged human beings. The economic advantages of empowering women are so vast as to persuade nations to move in that direction. Before long, we will consider sex slavery, honor killings, and acid attacks as unfathomable as foot-binding. The question is how long that transformation will take and how many girls will be kidnapped into brothels before it is complete—and whether each of us will be part of that historical movement, or a bystander.[4]

This is the question before each of us.

I scribe now to factor you into this revelation. It is my earnest prayer that my words will awaken something uncontainable hidden within you. I hope you will rise up with the strength of a lioness and bring God-wonder wherever you go. Then together we will be that force this world has never seen. Read on, my lioness sisters, and be awakened.

3

Dangerously Awake

Well-behaved women rarely make history.
LAUREL THATCHER ULRICH

In my quest to study the lioness, I read books and articles and watched DVDs, documentaries, and even YouTube clips in order to observe lionesses in different settings, stages, and interactions. Even though I had been on an African safari, my American vantage of the lioness was limited at best. Even now, I don't consider myself an expert on lionesses, but I am a fascinated observer.

One of the documentaries followed the resettlement of two lionesses and one lion into a newly designated reserve in South Africa. The lion was the pride's alpha male, and with the help of the two lionesses, he had successfully established his domain. Together the three of them reigned over a large portion of the South African reserve.

In order to follow the pride's movements and progress, a tracking collar had been placed on the male. After two years on the reserve, it was time to remove the collar. There was no longer any need to monitor the lion. In addition the collar hindered the fullness of his mane, and it had to come off so that his mane would appear as large as possible. (Lions use the width of each other's manes to visually gauge and determine whether to challenge the other for dominance of an area. If the adversary's mane appears too large for the challenger, meaning he would not be able to get his jaws around the other lion's throat, he will not proceed with a confrontation.)

The lion the rangers had collared two years earlier was no longer young, docile, or easily intimidated. He was mighty. With the help of the lionesses, he had successfully settled and defended the pride from encroachers and had repeatedly proven himself a seasoned protector. He would not be easily captured now that he had learned to roam wild, fearless, and free. The rangers would need to sedate him in order to remove the collar. They located the lion and, while maintaining a safe distance, shot him with a tranquilizer dart. The first one barely fazed him; he hardly flinched as he turned his majestic golden gaze their way. They fired again. The lion faltered and then lay down. The rangers snapped into action; their vehicle approached the fallen lion, cutting through brush and bouncing over rough terrain to where his massive, tawny form had dropped.

Just as they were about to jump off the Jeep and remove the collar, who should appear? The lion's alpha lioness—and she would have none of it. Because of a lioness's ability to all but disappear into her surroundings, the rangers had not detected her presence until she chose to appear before them. Their lack of awareness of her did not translate to her lack of awareness of them. As soon as she realized her lion was down, she rose and moved out of hiding into plain sight. She boldly made her presence known to the group of rangers. After inserting herself between the fallen lion and eager rangers, she growled menacingly while she paced back and forth in front of her mate. With flashing ears and raised fur, she let the men know she was not happy.

The rangers had a small window of time in which to get to the lion and remove the collar before the sedative wore off, but the lioness was making it impossible for them. The rangers had one remaining dose of tranquilizer. *To get to him, they would have to tranquilize her.* The marksman raised his gun again and took careful aim. When the dart hit, the enraged lioness turned toward the rangers, then fell down with the dart beneath her. As the team of rangers approached the sedated lion, the tension in the air was palpable. Like his lioness, he was incapacitated but not unconscious, and his eyes tracked their every move.

Speaking in whispers and reaching under the backside of the lion's mane, a ranger used a sharp hunting knife to cut the collar free and then removed the two sedative darts from the lion. Then the rangers moved away and turned their attention to the lioness. They had to move quickly before one or both of the huge cats recovered. The lioness lay on her side, revealing that the skin around her breasts had thickened, which meant she was pregnant. Gently and ever so carefully the rangers lifted her hindquarters and quickly removed the dart.

In the background the lion growled and struggled to arise, but he was still unable to gain his feet. The rangers swiftly made their way back into the vehicle, never turning their backs on the lions. The Jeep's engine started, and there was an audible exhale of relief as the group got under way. Dropping his formerly hushed tone, the narrator explained, "There's nothing more dangerous than being in the presence of lions when they are fully awake."

TRANQUILIZED CHRISTIANS

When I heard the pairing of the concepts "dangerous" and "fully awake," it got my attention. What would happen if, like the lions, we were dangerous and fully awake? Then and only then would we pose any threat to the darkness that holds so many captive.

Lovely ones, in this moment I pray we might each realize that we are truly frightening to our enemy and that he has done everything in his power to contain us. He knows he cannot get close enough to capture and chain us if we are fully awake and mobile. To counter, he sedates us so that we might not do the things God has called us to do. But like the lioness of my vision, we must wake up, rise up, remember who we are, and confront the evil in this world with light.

SEDATED BY THE DAY TO DAY

But make sure that you don't get so absorbed and exhausted in taking care of all your day-by-day obligations that you lose track of the time and doze off, oblivious to God. The night is about over, dawn is about to break. *Be up and awake to what God is doing!* God is putting the finishing touches on the salvation work he began when we first believed. We can't afford to waste a minute, must not squander these precious daylight hours in frivolity and indulgence, in sleeping around and dissipation, in bickering and grabbing everything in sight. Get out of bed and get dressed! Don't loiter and linger, waiting until the very last minute. Dress yourselves in Christ, and be up and about! (Romans 13:11–14)

Notice the word choices in this admonishment: don't get absorbed and exhausted by *your* daily obligations. They will rob the value of your time or cause you to fall asleep. These life scripts are an urgent charge to rise up and be alert and awake to what God is doing. When you are awake to what God is doing, then you will know what you are to do! The time for lingering is over. It is time to be up and about. The alarm went off hours ago!

This need for a good rousing was uniquely highlighted during a recent phone call with a friend. She told me how she and her husband had enjoyed a meal with a prominent rabbinical teacher. He bared his heart about how burdened he was for the plight of Jewish Americans. This rabbi travels and lectures in synagogues and conferences throughout our nation, imploring Jewish Americans to pray that American Christians will rise up together and realize their power to influence. He is concerned because the Jewish population of our country is far too small to stand on its own if Christians do not come alongside them as advocates to stem the anti-Semitic and anti-Christian tide rising against all of us.

Far too many of us are discouraged, sedated, or sadly unaware of what's really going on in the world. Could this be because for far too long we have heard a tranquilizing escapist gospel that motivates very few to save the lost? Has a lack of movement and spiritual exercise left us drowsy and lethargic? Has legalistic oppression or a casual attitude toward sin slowed our actions, causing our responses to be delayed or dulled? Could it be that God is in the process of shaking us in order to raise us up and make us dangerously awake? If so, it wouldn't be the first time.

The children of Israel wandered in the desert for many more years than necessary. They journeyed aimlessly, like an exceedingly large number of sheep. Sometimes they strayed and complained; other times they obediently followed the cloud by day and camped under the pillar of fire at night. Sometimes they listened to their shepherd, Moses; other times they didn't. But as they gathered to camp on the plains of Moab, which bordered their promised land, their assembled presence became evident. The surrounding nations were aware of their arrival. This pit stop of unskilled desert wanderers appeared to the inhabitants of the land as a gathering of mighty warriors.

No longer a collection of abused slaves, the Israelites had recaptured their identity as God's royalty (*Israel* means "prince of God"). After so many years of wandering in the wilderness, they were preparing to settle. Perhaps even then God's children missed what was so glaringly evident and apparent to the kings, the prophet Balaam, and to the enemy nations surrounding Israel. They were no longer wanderers but handpicked God-worshipers and warriors unaware.

Sadly, without an awareness of who they truly were and the correct perspective of who surrounded them (enemy nations), God's children lost vision and purpose. They cast off their former holy restraint and made a gaping judgment error. Before entering into the Promised Land, they foolishly formed some unholy alliances. Their mistake stands as our warning: there is danger if you wake up but have forgotten who you are.

To put it simply, they had an orgy in the desert. The men of Israel engaged in unbridled sex with the Moabite women who had been sent into their camp by the prophet Balaam's counsel (see Numbers 25:1–2; 31:16; Revelation 2:14). The women invited the Israelite men to be a part of Moab's sex/religion worship. The results were disastrous, and God's people were temporarily sidetracked. Before it was all over, there was a plague, a zealous priest, and a confirmed enemy—the Midianites. God instructed Moses to number the people, and then the people regrouped.

However, Israel's enemies could not triumph over them. When the Israelites were obedient, victory was secure, but whenever they moved outside God's directives, judgment overtook them. They repented, and God lifted the plague, but not before twenty-four thousand Israelites had died.

What's the lesson in this for us? If our enemy can't keep us sedated—still, docile, and inactive—then he will entice us to defile our places of rest and to engage in ungodly and perverse forms of worship. What do sedated Christians look like? They say and believe things like the following:

- "The world is going down the drain… I hope the Rapture happens soon so we can all escape."
- "Why shouldn't my husband and I watch instructional videos of other married couples having sex?"
- "It's all so frightening. I am going to cover my eyes *(yawn)*, and now that my eyes are closed, I think I'll take a nap."
- "God knows I am only human, and I have sexual needs that are not being fulfilled by my spouse. I know I shouldn't, but after all I am already forgiven…"
- "This isn't the president I voted for. I am not praying for him."
- "Sex and human trafficking is tragic, but it's an overseas problem, right?"
- "How sad that all those people died in earthquakes in Haiti and Chile. Isn't it great the celebrities are raising money to help?"

Sometimes I want to weep because I fear we've forgotten who we are. We are not our own; we are God's. We're a holy people set apart for him and his purposes. We are not some group of straggling, struggling, fatherless refugees who are overcome by sin and wondering if there is a God. We are the collective body of Christ, and as such we are destined for triumph, victory, and signs and wonders. Sadly, some of our sisters don't know that yet.

ANSWERS, NOT PROBLEMS

We have already briefly highlighted the dynamic I wrote about in 2005 in my book *Fight Like a Girl*—the premise that "you, daughter, are an answer, not a problem." As I complete *Lioness Arising*, an important and riveting book titled *Half the Sky* offers this confirmation: "Women aren't the problem but the solution."[1] This book was crafted by the husband-and-wife team of Nicholas D. Kristof and Sheryl WuDunn, Pulitzer Prize–winning journalists. They wrote with the intention of awakening the world to an urgent need to empower women with equal value, education, and economic opportunity. Their work has, thankfully, created quite a stir in the world community of actors, activists, and media.

I raise the issue again here because I am saddened that the church was not the first to confront gender inequality. It would appear we are like Jonah, the sleepy prophet of old who slumbered belowdecks in a dark hold while the crew manning the ship frantically tried to navigate a fatal storm. We should have been the first on deck and seeking God's solution to the glaring injustice tipping the balance of our world. But unlike Jonah we are not experiencing an isolated storm pummeling a single ocean vessel. The entire world is in upheaval as environmental storms pelt the earth and financial earthquakes destabilize world economies. Injustice is causing our earth to shake and sway. In an aroused state of alarm, people are turning to Christians and asking, "How did this happen?" The captive, hurting, and confused turn our way and ask how we can sleep when we should be crying out to God for a plan to be part of his intervention before it is too late. But far too many in the church have allowed the present motion to rock them into an uneasy sleep or to agitate them into arguing about what does not truly matter.

In Jonah's day, God sent a storm to awaken the prophet from his disobedience and to remind him the people of Nineveh were in a bad way. God never wants to leave people in harm's way, yet Jonah was loath to prevent the destruction that hovered over the ancient city. So he ran and hid in the hold of a ship. As he traveled in the opposite direction from where God had told him to go, he fell asleep. God sent a storm so mighty that the vessel that held Jonah was on the verge of being torn apart. Why did Jonah run? He didn't want to rescue those he deemed unworthy. Look at his conversation with God after both he and the city were spared.

Jonah was furious. He lost his temper. He yelled at GOD, "GOD! I knew it—when I was back home, I knew this was going to happen! That's why I ran off to Tarshish! I knew you were sheer grace and mercy, not easily angered, rich in love, and ready at the drop of a hat to turn your plans of punishment into a program of forgiveness! (Jonah 4:1–2)

Jonah wanted God to judge and punish the city, but God wanted to extend grace and mercy. Jonah was okay with God obliterating a city filled with people but upset enough to die over a shade tree that withered.

Then God said to Jonah, "What right do you have to get angry about this shade tree?"
Jonah said, "Plenty of right. It's made me angry enough to die!"
GOD said, "What's this? How is it that you can change your feelings from pleasure to anger overnight about a mere shade tree that you did nothing to get? You neither planted nor watered it. It grew

up one night and died the next night. So, why can't I likewise change what I feel about Nineveh from anger to pleasure, this big city of more than a hundred and twenty thousand childlike people who don't yet know right from wrong, to say nothing of all the innocent animals?" (Jonah 4:9–11)

Hello! Have we likewise lost our perspective of what is important to God? Are we more concerned with our comfort and shelter than with what God values? The Most High is not up in heaven excited by the prospect of destruction. He longs to rescue all who are in a bad way! Let's not hold back hope from the very ones God wants to save. I pray that you will allow God to awaken the lioness within you and to position you to rescue—not judge—others from the evil that threatens to overcome and destroy them.

It is time to obey God's summons. He entrusted us with the message of good news for the earth. He commanded that we love one another. He charged us to care for widows, orphans, aliens, and the poor. Even now he encourages daughters young and old to bring our solutions to the world's problems. He invites us to lay aside our differences and labor together in the work of God.

Some of us are still working on being kind to one another. Others are too busy crying over losses. And far too many fight over silly doctrinal issues, crying out against other parts of Christ's body.

Lovely ones, I don't want our wake-up call to require an overboard toss like Jonah's or a sojourn in a wilderness like the Israelites'! So let's look at the evil and problems in the world and allow them to shake us awake. In my spirit I see a people aroused, agitated, and ready to change their world.

YOUR UNIQUE EXPRESSION

As I have been writing this book, my editors have encouraged me to share examples of women who are fully awake so that you might see what a woman who is fully awake can accomplish. But I don't want to limit it to what we've seen. This story of the fully awake and dangerous is still being written. I believe the world has yet to see what it looks like when Christian women, individually and collectively, are fully awake and dangerous.

Twice God gave me the charge to begin the *wake-up process* in Christian women. I have no idea what all this may look like once we are *fully awake,* but I am pretty sure we will look dangerous in the dark and glorious in the light. As I have contemplated this further, I have come to believe that the expression of a fierce, wild lioness of a Christian woman is yet to be defined.

I have also come to the realization that people like to be told what to do. But a how-to, step-by-step Christianity leaves us void of much of the mystery of God. So this is not a how-to message. I want *you* awakened—to rise up a lioness and walk in your unique expression of what that means. Only you and God can define what that lioness will look like when she is fully awake in you.

I recently asked my staff to pass on words or images that a lioness awakens or arouses in them. I wasn't surprised when their answers ranged all the way from *grace* and *tenderness* to *fierce* and *fearless.* This is how varied and vast this wake-up response has the potential of being.

As I've searched the Scriptures, I have found that God often says to his people or his prophets, "Go there, do this, say that," without any clear indication of what will happen next. An example of this is Elisha, who told a widow to "borrow jugs and bowls from all your neighbors. And not just a few—all you can get. Then come home and lock the door behind you, you and your sons. Pour oil into each container; when each is full, set it aside" (2 Kings 4:3–4). This seems a bit random. How was this going to solve the problem of debt collectors threatening to enslave this woman's sons? Well, when she had done what she was told, she returned to the man of God, and he told her to "sell the oil and make good on your debts. Live, both you and your sons, on what's left" (2 Kings 4:7).

I wonder how much miraculous provision we miss because we want to know steps two, three, and four even before we have completed step one. So think of this as a "read the words, pray, and allow God to pour himself into all the vessels you've laid out before him" type of book. Ask God to fill your mind with the idea of a lioness in whatever shape, form, or container he wants to use to inspire you.

Don't be afraid of the imagery of us as lionesses or Jesus as a lion. This is not unlike the representation of Jesus as our shepherd and how he relates to us, his sheep. Are we literal sheep, or does God ask us to follow and trust him as such? Likewise, Jesus is our bridegroom, and we are his collective bride. It's an allegorical picture. Jesus is at once Shepherd, King, God, Man, Bridegroom, Brother, Lion, Lamb, as well as the Beginning and the End. Is it surprising that he might want to stretch us? My intent is to allow you to respond out of your unique perceptions and place of strength and influence.

WAKE-UP DUTY

When I was in college, my sorority house had a sleeping porch. I'm not sure why it was called this because it was not outside the building, nor did it have any outside access. It was a long, darkened, second-story room filled with bunk beds. Some were arranged along the wall, while others stood in ranks perpendicular to a row of darkened windows.

Because so many of us shared this common room, we weren't allowed alarm clocks. Instead, we rotated the assignment of my least favorite chore: wake-up duty. Before retiring each night, the sisters would move their nametags to the time slots for when they wanted to be awakened. This meant the person with wake-up duty had to know where each of her sisters slept. On the night before her morning wake-up detail, she slept outside the group in another room where it was all right to set an alarm.

When it was my turn, I would set the alarm for a half hour before the earliest designated time so I could shower. Taking a shower without waiting in line was the only benefit of being the first one up.

Once the wake-up process began, I made the rounds, waking girls at fifteen-minute to half-hour intervals for the next two to three hours. I slipped in and out of the darkened sleeping porch while trying to eat and finish getting ready myself. Time and again I'd creep in quietly, close the door, then grope my way in the dark, counting the bunks carefully in an effort not to wake up the sleeping sisters as I moved among them. When I found the designated sister or sisters, I gently but firmly woke them.

There was such a sense of responsibility, because I knew every one of the sisters was depending on me to rouse her. There were classes to attend, tests to be taken, reviews that couldn't be missed, and, of course, boyfriends to meet up with.

I had blown a wake-up once when I was a pledge. I had been too quiet, too gentle, and I was hesitant to shake a senior sister. She had mumbled a reply, and I assumed she was awake, but she wasn't. She was merely talking in her sleep. At lunch that day she read me the riot act and let me know what my lack of effectiveness had cost her. There are some mistakes you are not willing to make twice. So I learned quickly there were some sisters who required a good shaking, others who responded to a gentle touch, and some who sat up wide-awake when a sister merely whispered their name. Some sisters thanked me; others cussed and ordered me away.

The trickiest were those who appeared awake and even said, "Okay, okay, I'm awake," and then went back to sleep. I learned that this type of sleepy sister required me to stay at the post until she was off her bunk with both feet on the floor.

Another dilemma came in waking the wrong sister. Even though I tried to be quiet and careful, sometimes I'd wake a sister in the bunk above or beside. She'd sit up, startle me by grabbing my arm, and whisper, "Hey, I'm awake. Take my name off the wake-up list!"

I'm ashamed to say it, but back then I was one of the cussing, difficult-to-wake-up types. I almost consistently required a second wake-up call. Having done the duty, I knew the rules. If a sister was awakened twice but still remained in bed, I was not required to wake her a third time. This dynamic added an urgency to the second wake-up call, because you knew it would be your last. Once my sisters were awake and moving, I was no longer responsible to monitor them. They were sisters in motion. I had to finish getting myself dressed.

Our generous God does not operate under the rules of my sorority. He is more than happy to continue wake-up calls until the very last minute, yet there is no denying the urgency. I sense that even now some sisters are responding to the wake-up calls issued to the sleepy women around them.

AWAKEN SOMETHING FIERCE

I think it is funny that in this season of life I am again doing wake-up duty, only this time much more is at stake. Sometimes it feels as though I am still wandering among bunks in darkened rooms where I gently shake, stubbornly stay, and at times—glorious times—merely whisper my sisters' names, and they awaken and arise.

I know I am not alone in this wake-up task, and each of God's daughters will respond to different means and methods of stimuli to wake her from her slumber. In my case, I'm charged to put some wild principles and beautiful imagery before you. It is my prayer that this revelation of compelling majesty and strength will have the power to awaken something fierce in you so that when you are fully awake, you will know what to do.

The world needs you, lovely lioness sister, not to merely wake up, but to give expression to your God-given, fierce side. What does it look like for a Christian woman to be *fierce*? Is it yelling and screaming, clawing and kicking? There might be a time for that. I know that if any of my children or grandchildren were being attacked, that and more would be my reaction. God actually refers to this mama bear–lioness reaction in the book of Hosea and claims it as one of his own.

Like a bear whose cubs have been taken away,
   I will tear out your heart.
I will devour you like a hungry lioness
   and mangle you like a wild animal. (Hosea 13:8, NLT)

Yikes! This verse definitely captures the ferocious, violent side of *fierce*, but there is more than mangling violence to be found in this intense word. Other words, which round out the meaning of *fierce*, include *intense, strong, powerful, turbulent, forceful, ardent,* and *aggressive*. I cannot imagine a collection of words that more accurately captures what I feel stirring within me. Without a doubt something turbulent has been awakened that has brought with it greater clarity and power, as though a storm was collecting strength.

This force hasn't caused personal turmoil; it has brought focus. With greater focus, I've found myself increasingly passionate about things of which I was formerly unaware.

Many of these moments of awakening have caught me a bit off guard. One came in late October or early November of 2007. I was in the bathroom, of all places, reading a magazine. As I turned the pages, I read for the first time about the atrocities of sex trafficking in Thailand. I finished the article and reread certain paragraphs, almost unable to believe that what I was reading was true. Could people really be this cruel? Could this be happening and I be unaware? I began to cry (in the bathroom, of all places), and then I prayed, *God, if there is any strength or voice I can lend to this issue, I am your girl.* With this prayerful wake-up, something shifted.

A few weeks passed, and then I received a phone call from Life Outreach. "Lisa, we are putting a team together to go to Thailand to raise funds and awareness to prevent sex trafficking, and you were the person we thought of sending." Three months later I was on my way to Thailand as part of Life Outreach's first initiative against human trafficking.

What if I hadn't prayed that day? What if I had cried, shaken my head, and continued turning pages? Before long I would have been looking at the newest skin-care breakthrough, fashion trend, or diet secret. If I had read on rather than prayed, chances are I would have gone to bed that night without ever lifting my voice to heaven. When the issue came to my attention again, I might have said something like, "Yeah, I heard about that... Read it in a magazine... That is so, so sad."

But when you are *awakened,* you can't help but *respond.* Don't confuse being awakened with being upset. If something upsets you, you may react in that moment, but being upset about something doesn't have the power to keep you from turning pages. You can be upset and not awake. But you can't be fully awake, and therefore alertly aware of the problems in the world, and not respond. That's why when I read about young girls being kidnapped and thrown into brothels, I had to pray, telling God I would do whatever he wanted me to do to confront this atrocity. My prayer highlighted the opportunity when it came. Would there have been other opportunities? Perhaps, but that one might have been missed.

God Did Not Save You to Tame You

God does not reveal himself as limitless in order to limit us. Quite the contrary. He wants to put his heart within us. My friend Christine says it best: "God did not save you to tame you!"

God is not looking for people who act like Christians. He wants us to *be* Christians! The word *Christian* means "anointed or Christlike one." Jesus did not go around "being good"; he went around "doing good" and releasing all who were oppressed. What has he anointed you to do?

> God's Spirit is on me;
> > he's chosen me to preach the Message of good news to the poor,
> Sent me to announce pardon to prisoners and
> > recovery of sight to the blind,
> To set the burdened and battered free,
> > to announce, *This is God's year to act!*" (Luke 4:18–19)

If the Spirit of God was placed on Jesus to do all these things, and if we are born of this same Spirit, then we are to do as he did—preach the good news to the poor, set the burdened and battered free, and announce, "This is God's year to act!" I believe that each and every year is God's year to act, that he is still waiting for us to go into motion on his behalf.

In light of this charge, God does not need a band of domesticated daughters who spend their days baking and behaving well. Nothing wrong with baking, but if that is all we do, God won't use us to change history.

> **Well-behaved women rarely make history.**
>
> —Laurel Thatcher Ulrich

I know this quote may challenge some of you. It challenged me when I first read it. This is not an admonition to be naughty but to realize that change often comes with the challenge of the status quo.

In the eyes of her southern culture and the bus company, Rosa Parks was not behaving well when she refused to yield her seat and move to the designated "colored" section in the back of the bus. One woman's choice to hold her ground and not change seats changed how our nation looked at racial segregation. I seriously doubt in that moment she realized she was making history. Time alone has the power to reveal motives and consequence of choices. Maybe Rosa was just tired of being marginalized and denied her God-given right of human dignity.

What about Deborah, Jael, Tamar, Esther, Bathsheba, Abigail, Rahab, and even Mary? (These are just a biblical sampling, because there are more.)

Was Deborah behaving well by inciting her people against a dominant oppressor and riding into war with the men? The leaders of her time thought not. An army rose to oppose her rebellion, but they could not prevail. When the God-chosen male leader, Barak, hesitated, Deborah carried out God's directive the best she knew how.

What of Jael? Did she have to use a tent peg to kill her enemy? Couldn't she just have turned him over to the authorities while he slept? Possibly, but she didn't. God was okay with her choice, and a song was composed to declare her valor.

Then there is Tamar. This twice-widowed woman pretended to be a prostitute and slept with her widowered father-in-law, patriarch Judah. Her behavior is shocking on many levels. There is no evidence that God instructed her to do this. She chose this course of action. But the son of this tenacious woman is found in the lineage of Christ, and she was declared righteous.

Esther disobeyed the command to come to the king only when called. Disobedience had gotten Vashti, Xerxes' first wife, sacked. Esther should have known better! But her choice to behave badly at court saved her people.

Bathsheba was an adulteress and the mother of Solomon the wise. Rahab was a prostitute who lied to her king and hid enemy spies. Not only did her actions of faith redeem her family from the destruction of Jericho, but her son is in the lineage of David and Jesus. Abigail circumvented her husband. Her choice saved her household and won her the heart of King David.

Mary appeared to carry a illegitimate child and gave birth to the Son of God. What if she had said, "Unwed and pregnant will look bad. Can this wait until I'm married so I will look well behaved?"

History alone justifies the choices of these women. Their hearts were awakened and stirred.

How will you respond when you are fully, dangerously awake? What history will you make? Will you, like the fierce lioness, awaken from a tranquilized state and rise up to defend your family, your community, your world? Are you awake? Even now, what is stirring in your heart?

4

The Sum of Fear and Wonder

I am fearfully and wonderfully made;
Marvelous are Your works.

PSALM 139:14, NKJV

Lionesses are strong and sleek. They move with muscled purpose, aware that their existence and the survival of their young depend on a legacy of skill and strength. Their fur ripples when they walk. Unlike us, they are not concerned with whether their skin is sagging or if their tails are too long or even that they all look alike. They are comfortable in their skin.

Lionesses are stunning.

Having observed them in the wild, I believe they actually *know* this. The contrast of how we view ourselves and how the lioness perceives herself might be captured if humans and lionesses could converse. For a moment let's pretend we can speak to one another.

"Lioness, you are stunning."

The lioness responds, "I know. Do you want to see what I can do?"

Thrilled, we answer, "Yes."

"See my paw," she invites. "Watch this."

We are awed as the lioness releases her claws from an upturned paw.

"With this paw I can take down a gazelle that will nourish my young and feed the members of my pride. Note this." She retracts her claws, and the paw is velvet again. "With this paw, I play with the young and train them to be mighty."

We nod and look down at our nails, noticing that the polish on them is chipped.

The lioness speaks again. "Behold my teeth!"

We draw back, awed by teeth so varied and sharp.

"With these teeth I defend, kill, and eat, yet these same teeth carry the young from one place to another without harming them."

We nod, noting the contrast.

Then our lioness sighs contentedly as she sums up her beauty: "I am fearfully and wonderfully made."

Indeed, we can agree; she is the living sum of fear and wonder.

But wait…so are you.

I am fearfully and wonderfully made;
> Marvelous are Your works. (Psalm 139:14, NKJV)

I dare you to say this out loud now that you have the context of the lioness. Honestly, lovely one, you are a marvelous work of God, and so are the men and women around you. It is just that too many of us have forgotten that the dynamic of marvel does not end when we exit the womb.

When was the last time you had a conversation with a woman that sounded remotely like the one with our lioness?

The following is more likely an example of what you might hear when one woman speaks to another.

"You are beautiful."

"Thank you, but actually I haven't lost all the weight I gained from having my last child."

Any woman who has birthed a child (or watched another woman birth a child) should realize we are indeed fearfully and wonderfully made. Somehow we have lost sight of this, but the lioness has not. She knows her beauty is revealed in her strength. It is captured in what her body can actually do, not merely in how it looks. *Her attractiveness is undeniable, because her power is unquestionable.* She knows what her body is capable of, and she revels in the wonder of it. The reveling of the lioness brings glory to her Creator. She is powerful and skillful, and she trains the young of her pride to be the same.

It is important we remember the beauty of strength and function. I am not referring to being physically thinner. I am referring to being physically and spiritually aware and sharp—focused—and thus ready for whatever task God has for us. If we are to be true lionesses, we must have strength. Not long ago I discovered just how easy it is for us to be mistaken about how strong we really are.

MISTAKEN FOR BUFF

Here is how my week-long delusion began. I was tired after completing a series of meetings in the land down under. The five meetings were over, and it was Sunday night and wind-down time. I was invited to meet with the conference leadership team, who'd worked tirelessly to pull the event together. We were all a bit silly and slaphappy due to the heady combination of lack of sleep, abundance of food, and the goodness of God.

In this relaxed state, one of the leaders shared her takeaway and insights with me, and said, "You know, around here they call me 'the nailer.' And today during the Sunday morning service, I nailed who it is you remind me of."

"Who?" I asked.

Without a moment's hesitation she declared, "You look like the *original* Sarah Connor."

There was a long pause as I processed this.

"Wait…wasn't she a blonde?" I countered, unconvinced.

"Yeah, yeah, it's not her hair." She shook her head and waved a hand dismissively. "It's her face structure and her stance and her like, like…buffness," she explained as she traced her jaw line and assumed an intimidating stance.

Did she just say "buffness"?

Okay, that is not even a real word, but she had my full attention. Even if the comparison was a stretch, I now wanted to look like this Sarah Connor! I nodded, unwilling to dismiss any idea or image that represented me as buff. I would leave well enough alone, and when I got back to the States, I would look up this buff woman from the movie *The Terminator.*

Once home I enlisted the help of my son Alec, the media whiz.

"Can you find me the original Sarah Connor? I need to see her. People are saying I look like her," I offered.

He was doubtful, but he located a poster of Sarah Connor sporting a tank top and little round sunglasses and wielding a shotgun. Sure enough. She looked fierce, honed, and more than cut. I can't say I immediately saw her maternal side. (This was important to me because I speak on topics like nurture and mothering.) But then again, isn't maternal relative to your situation?

What could be more maternal than being buff and knowing how to handle a gun if your life purpose is to protect your son from robotic assassins?

Alec also found a compilation of video clips. I fear this cheesy 1980s montage pushed me over the edge. The mosaic featured Sarah Connor riding a motorcycle, loading a shotgun with one arm, and doing pull-ups on her overturned twin bed in a mental hospital room. In that moment I was her!

I could have put an end to my confusion right then and there if I'd asked myself a simple question: *Lisa, have you ever done a pull-up?*

But I didn't. Instead, I let my imagination run wild. As I watched Sarah Connor do pull-ups, I imagined that my arms were just as strong and, given the right motivation, that I could do pull-ups just like her. Surely I was *nearly* as buff as she appeared. Never mind *the fact* that even when I was in peak physical condition, I could barely do the flexed-arm hang for the president's physical fitness test in high school. (I only lasted by imagining myself suspended over crocodiles.)

Somehow I'd forgotten I had injured both of my shoulders—one skiing and the other in an incident too wimpy to explain.

Come to think of it, I'd *never* done a pull-up! But none of this mattered. In that moment if Sarah did it, I could do it.

Not only did I want to look like her; now I wanted to act like her. Why was the first female action hero working out? When the moment of her release came, she would be strong and ready to rescue and protect her son. Wow! I love women who know how to use seasons of hardship to gain strength. Sarah and me? Why, we were almost sisters.

In the middle of this delusion, I did something I'd never done.

I dialed Gold's Gym.

I remembered hearing about an amazing trainer and asked for him by name. The receptionist at the gym patched me through. I could barely contain my excitement as I asked if Robert had any openings that very day. I imagined a few private training sessions—three, maybe four, tops—and Sarah and I would be twins. Yes, twins…with a different hair color because I drew the line at going blond, but I was willing to work out so that our chiseled, buff arms could reflect each other.

Robert agreed to see me in a few hours for an assessment.

The word *assessment* should have given me reason to pause, but it didn't. I hung up the phone, energized, and I asked Alec to make me a workout mix of clean songs with driving beats. When that was finished, I announced, "I am going to the gym. Who wants to go with me?"

Two surprised sons appeared, and we headed out to the gym. With my newly loaded iPod, I'd be bumping as I strolled into the gym. Perhaps next time I would don a tank top and make it easier for my trainer to make the Sarah Connor connection.

In my excitement I arrived a bit early and saw my future trainer in the distance. He was going to be so pleased to meet his new protégée. No doubt he would be both excited and relieved to train someone already so close to her goal.

Or so I imagined.

Robert was working with a client and waved me toward the treadmill to warm up. My machine granted me an elevated angle, and I noticed his client was a woman who appeared to be close to my age. And anything I imagined I was…she was!

Not only chiseled, she was tan. She looked very Sarah-ish in her tank top and camo pants. In that moment I experienced my first in a series of sinking feelings. I examined my arms in the reality of the fluorescent gym lights and noted they looked flaccid, pale, and slightly green.

Wait a minute! I was not going to be intimidated. If my schedule opened up a bit, I could be tan too. In defiance, I upped the treadmill pace a few notches. The buff me was in hiding, simply waiting to be revealed. A few training sessions and some time in the sun, and I would be that woman. After all, was Sarah tanning in her prison cell?

I looked away, turned on my iPod, and started walking in earnest.

It wasn't long before my trainer came by and smiled encouragingly. "Go ahead and do fifteen minutes, then we'll meet to discuss your goals. I'm still wrapping up with a client."

Fifteen minutes? Was he serious? I remembered reading that eight minutes was all anyone ever needed. But I did not want to disappoint or correct my trainer on our first day together, so I just smiled and complied.

When my fifteen minutes were up, I slipped off the machine and headed to the women's locker room to locate the scales. I had forgotten to weigh myself and assumed that was information he would need. This meant walking past the truly buff woman. As I passed, she called out to me.

"Hey, are you working out with Robert?" she asked breathlessly.

I nodded as I sipped nonchalantly from my water bottle.

"He's killing me!" she gasped as she continued her trek on the stair-climbing machine. "I'm used to working out, but Robert is a whole 'nother level."

I stopped in my tracks. "But you're buff…"

She shook her head as though answering me took more strength than she could muster right then.

Robert called my name from across the gym and waved me over to his cubicle. I approached quite a bit less confidently than I'd entered the gym.

"I was just going to weigh myself," I mumbled.

But he wasn't interested in my weight. Robert wanted to know how strong I was.

"Did you bring a towel?" he asked.

"No," I answered and then explained that I rarely sweat when I work out. Looking back, it probably would have been more accurate to simply say I rarely worked out.

SKINNY FAT

I can't remember exactly how the process of humiliation went down, but here's my best recollection. I was escorted to the epicenter of the gym rather than to the private room that I had assumed all assessments took place in. When we reached an area of cleared floor space, Robert instructed me to give him ten.

I knew he meant push-ups. I just wasn't sure what kind he wanted.

"You mean the girl kind on my knees, right?"

"No, regular ones." He answered in a detached manner as he lifted his clipboard and raised his pencil menacingly.

I dropped and did ten sloppy, shaky, badly formed push-ups.

With no time allotment for a break, a bonding moment, or a "Way to go, Lisa!" he added, "Now twenty-five jumping jacks."

I panicked. I knew jumping jacks were easy, but I couldn't remember how to do them.

"Do my hands touch at the top?" I asked.

Robert didn't answer.

I did what I thought was twenty-five jumping jacks. As I bounced awkwardly, I noticed I was drawing the attention of other gym members. Even my sons were shaking their heads and laughing as they looked my way.

"Drop and give me another ten," said Robert.

Out of breath and stalling for time, I asked, "Do you mean push-ups this time or lunges or something else?"

"Push-ups," he answered.

I dropped, but this time was even harder. My arms were shaking. They were pitiful, and I more or less bounced my belly up and down.

Robert reserved comment. "Another twenty-five jumping jacks."

I wanted to do them correctly this time, so I asked again, "Do my hands touch at the top?" My voice sounded surprisingly stressed.

"It doesn't matter… Go," he ordered.

Well, it mattered to me! And it mattered to my sons, who were shrinking in embarrassment as their mother flubbed jumping jacks in front of the entire gym.

But this was just the beginning of my agony. It was off to the next very public area, where I would attempt leg lifts in a chair. I knew how to do this one.

I mounted the frame and waited for instructions.

"I want fifteen leg lifts."

I lifted my knees waist level, all the while thinking my form was admirable.

"No, not like that," Robert ordered. "I want your legs straight out…and lift them this high." He suspended his hand higher than my waist.

I swung my legs up as high as I could but couldn't reach his hand.

"Higher," he encouraged.

Was this a joke? Fifteen? I couldn't even do one. I managed to hit his hand a few times—okay, maybe zero times—but I think he was moving his hand up!

I believe free weights were next, but in my memory it's all a blur. I took a seat on the bench while Robert chose a pair of free weights. He came back with a pair of three-pound weights. I smiled. This time I would surprise him with my strength.

"Robert, I normally curl the twelve-and-a-half-pound weights," I explained.

"Let's just try these first," Robert countered.

I took the weights in my sweaty, shaking hands.

"Lift them like this for me."

I nodded knowingly.

I hefted them easily.

"No, not like that. Like this," he said as he repositioned my arm slightly. "All the way up and all the way down."

Something was wrong. I couldn't lift the weights more than a few inches! It was probably the push-ups, because my arms were not working. I lowered my arms and tried again. I still couldn't lift the weights more than an inch or two. I looked at Robert in shock, but he was already turning to get a pair of lighter weights. Actually the lightest the gym possessed. How could this be?

"Honestly, I normally lift twelve-pound weights…sometimes even fifteen," I stammered.

"You've been lifting wrong," he concluded.

When the agony was finally over, Robert led me back to the cubicle. My chest was heaving, my legs were shaky, and my image of myself as Sarah Connor was completely shot!

I had not passed one single part of the physical assessment.

Solemnly, Robert started a chart. He asked me for my weight and then recorded the numbers. He asked about any injuries and marked the unisex figure on the sheet. I explained I was having challenges with my left knee and left shoulder. My injuries were noted. Then he handed me my nemesis—a handheld device that looked innocently like a Nintendo controller.

"Hold this in front of you with both hands," Robert instructed. "It will send an electrical current through your body and give an accurate reading of your fat percentage."

He pushed the start button, and there was a brief pause before a number appeared on the LED screen.

I was not completely surprised, but Robert was shocked by how high my actual fat percentage was.

"Perhaps I wasn't holding it right," I offered.

We repeated the process, and somehow the fat percentage increased by 1 percent.

"Maybe it's broken or I'm dehydrated."

About that time Alec wandered into the cubicle.

"Can I try it?" he asked.

Boom. His fat percentage was a trim 5.2 percent.

"What was yours, Mom?"

Without answering I waved him out of the cubicle.

Shaking his head, Robert pulled out a sheet of paper with two pictures on it. It looked like cross sections of steak. One was lean, one was not. I was the "not" picture.

"You're what we affectionately call 'Skinny Fat,'" he said.

I was horrified and immediately began to protest that I was a very active, possibly too busy person. I was not going to sit back in this plastic gym chair and allow the label of couch potato to be assigned to me!

Robert nodded knowingly. "Because you are active and going all the time, you are probably not eating enough protein to sustain the energy your body requires, so your body is burning your muscle for energy rather than your fat."

Noting my shock, he continued, "It's like eating a steak. What do you do? You cut off the fat, then eat the meat. Your body is the same. It is eating the meat, which is your muscle, and when you lose muscle, you lose strength. The only way you can get it back is through resistance training, which rebuilds your muscle."

He added insult to my injury by pointing out a few women who were considerably larger than me and told me that even though everyone else might think their fat percentage was higher, mine was probably higher than theirs! He also determined that the majority of my fat (now I am getting really vulnerable here!) was not in my midsection or my thighs. It was in my arms!

Sadly, the place where I had imagined I was most buff was my worst area!

All images of Sarah Connor and me doing pull-ups together were gone. The real choice was now before me. Did I want to continue to burn muscle and cripple my future potential of strength? Was I happy with the title "Skinny Fat" or "Fake Buff," or was I ready to become truly strong? In the midst of my embarrassment, I determined to be strong! For me it was never about looking good in clothes. Skinny fat accomplishes that. Rather it was about locating weakness and turning vulnerable body areas into sources of energy and power.

I didn't need to lose weight; I needed to gain strength.

I realized that weight alone was not an accurate reflection of my composition. What was I made of? When push came to shove, would I have the strength to stand the test? I could sprint for short spurts as long as there was no incline. But if distance or resistance was added, I caved. Why? Because I was too weak to bear the load of added weight.

I could lift only small amounts of weight, from limited stances. This is why I couldn't lift when Robert had the weight in a different position. My strength failed when he isolated a muscle group that was weak and vulnerable from lack of use.

There has been such a change in my attitude that, even as I type these words, I almost have to fight the urge to go work out. I went to the gym to be affirmed that I was buff, not to hear that I was weak. I did not like what I heard. But how wonderful to know the truth and to allow it to work its way into my life so I can make my weak places strong! Now there is a part of me that *wants* to realize my weakness so I might discover how to become strong.

I will not be able to locate these areas on my own. I'll need a trainer of sorts, which will mean a bit of expense and a lot of pain.

A PEOPLE INVINCIBLE

After this encounter I began to wonder how many of us are skinny fat—not physically, but spiritually. We look trim, but if too much weight is added to our lives, we cannot bear it. We do okay walking on flat surfaces at a comfortable pace. But life is not a treadmill that we control. We are on a path with God, and I sense the incline and speed increasing.

Why have I shared all this with you? Because I believe the body of Christ is on the verge of a total body makeover and an invincible uprising. But this idea is not mine alone. God says:

> On your feet, Daughter of Zion! Be threshed of chaff,
>   be refined of dross.
> I'm remaking you into a people invincible. (Micah 4:13)

Notice God didn't say invisible. He said invincible! His daughters are to have a presence of might on this earth. How long has it been since you felt invincible? Perhaps it was long, long ago when you ran and played as a little girl. You are not meant to hide in the dark and hope for an escape. You are meant to be a bearer of light and hope. You are meant to be an unbeatable, unconquerable, and unshakable daughter of Zion. Even now I hear, "Rise up, daughter, find your feet again! God wants you—invincible."

More often than not we develop spiritual strength from times of threshing and refining. Micah 4 helps us understand what this weight-bearing workout might look like:

> GOD will give you new life again.
>   He'll redeem you from your enemies.
>
> But for right now, they're ganged up against you,
>   many godless peoples, saying,
> "Kick her when she's down! Violate her!
>   We want to see Zion grovel in the dirt."
> These blasphemers have no idea
>   what GOD is thinking and doing in this.
> They don't know that this is the making of GOD's people,
>   that they are wheat being threshed, gold being refined.
>   (verses 10–12)

I love the promise in this passage. When you are down, when it seems your enemies are closing in for the kill, God is at work, refining you as gold. God uses hardship as a catalyst for making his people pure, precious, and sustainable.

Sometimes when media or individuals criticize Christians, there's a bit of truth to what they say. We should meet these critiques with humility and evaluate them to assess what is true in them. If someone says we are harsh, judgmental, or unloving, rather than reject this assessment outright, we should take a look at ourselves in light of God's Word. We should check ourselves and apologize if there is need.

Then there are the outrageous accusations of our enemy, the devil. At times his attacks are outright lies, such as when our Lord is blasphemed. Other times his attacks are pure evil, such as when God's children are told to denounce their Lord or be put to death (imagine the Inquisition here). These assaults are not to be negotiated with but overcome by bold declarations of truth and God's faithfulness. We see this illustrated in the book of Revelation:

> They defeated him through the blood of the Lamb
>   and the bold word of their witness.
> They weren't in love with themselves;
>   they were willing to die for Christ. (12:11)

As I read Micah 4:13, it was as though I heard God yell, "Enough! You thought you had destroyed my people, but you haven't. Instead, you've prepared them!" Israel is our example. When the Israelites strayed, their enemies rose in strength against them, and this hardship worked a refining in their lives. And just when the enemies imagined they had won, God revealed his people—remade and triumphant.

BETRAYED BY BUSY

So how do we begin this strength training? We begin with an honest assessment of our corporate and individual spiritual condition. The term *skinny fat* almost seems kind in comparison to the words of Trainer Jesus. Have you read his assessments from the book of Revelation? Only two of the seven churches passed his rigorous test of their strength. Here are two of the evaluations of those that didn't:

I see right through your work. You have a reputation for vigor and zest, but you're dead, stone dead.

Up on your feet! Take a deep breath! Maybe there's life in you yet. But I wouldn't know it by looking at your busywork; nothing of God's work has been completed. Your condition is desperate. Think of the gift you once had in your hands, the Message you heard with your ears—grasp it again and turn back to God. (3:1–3)

Just as all my physical activity decreased rather than increased my muscle strength, so spiritual busyness does not build spiritual strength. It distracts and drains us from God's work. Again Jesus charts the progress of the church:

I know you inside and out, and find little to my liking. You're not cold, you're not hot—far better to be either cold or hot! You're stale. You're stagnant. You make me want to vomit. You brag, "I'm rich, I've got it made, I need nothing from anyone," oblivious that in fact you're a pitiful, blind beggar, threadbare and homeless. (3:15–17)

What is this? God is calling people who live in houses homeless and rich people stale and stagnant? Both groups of people saw themselves one way, only to have Jesus shock them with a revelation of their true condition. Why would our Good Shepherd be so…well, harsh? He answers this question himself:

The people I love, I call to account—prod and correct and guide so that they'll live at their best. Up on your feet, then! About face! Run after God! (3:19)

God is honest about our spiritual condition because he loves us. He trains us so we can live life at our optimum level. To accomplish this transformation, Jesus is willing to shock us into true action. There is no need to respond to his admonition with shame, guilt, or condemnation. Instead, let's find our feet, turn around, and run hard after God.

BALANCING THE LOAD

I mentioned earlier that my left shoulder and knee were troubling me. During my assessment I learned why. They were acting up because every time I went on a trip I carried my bags on board, using almost exclusively the left side of my body. With rest, my left shoulder and knee were allowed to heal, and with exercise my left side grew stronger. By using both sides of my body to carry my bags and computer, I brought my body back into balance. How many of us are injured spiritually because we drag baggage or use only one side of our body to carry the load? This not only reflects the need for both men and women, or both sides of the body of Christ, to shoulder the weight, but it also shows how we as individuals should strengthen our whole person—our spirit, mind, and body. It is time we stop guarding old injuries and move forward with God.

In Psalm 144, God paints a beautiful picture of what it looks like when his sons and daughters both carry some weight and bear the load, spiritually speaking.

That our sons may be as plants grown up in their youth;

That our daughters may be as pillars, sculptured in palace style.

(verse 12, NKJV)

The New Living Translation says, "May our sons *flourish in their youth.*" Think of this: a generation of sons who are flourishing, which means increasing, prospering, booming, and even flaunting the goodness of God while they are yet young. What a contrast to what we have been trained to expect: males in their teens and twenties who squander the strength and vitality of their youth.

Daughters are described here as pillars. I looked up the definition of *pillar* and discovered it has two core meanings: the first describes a system of *support,* such as a column, post, mast, prop, or stake. The second primary definition of *pillar* is "leader." Under this noun I found all the same words listed above.

I believe that God is painting an architectural picture of his house in this passage. Are we women ready to be used for more than decoration? Are we ready to hold up the roof of God's house?

Which brings us back to the issue of strength and the training required to attain it.

Run to win. All good athletes train hard. They do it for a gold medal that tarnishes and fades. You're after one that's gold eternally.

I don't know about you, but I'm running hard for the finish line. I'm giving it everything I've got. No sloppy living for me! I'm staying alert and in top condition. I'm not going to get caught napping, telling everyone else all about it and then missing out myself. (1 Corinthians 9:24–27)

SETTING ASIDE FORMER LIMITATIONS

I have never been a good athlete. In high school I swam on the swim team because I loved water, lasagna, and sleepovers, but I never swam to win. I only swam to finish. I was content with third or fourth place. I just didn't want to be last. I hated swim meets so much that I would become ill before each event. To gain composure I would tell myself, *Just swim hard for a minute. Then it will be over, and you can go back to your friends.*

Sadly, I never realized my team needed me. I only thought of myself—my fears, my lack of drive. Because I never thought of my teammates, I never pushed myself. I never expected to win, so I never did. I was not an asset to my team; I was a liability. Looking back, I believe I was more afraid of winning than I was of losing. If I excelled, then I would have to keep excelling, and I was not willing to pay the price to do that. I was also afraid that if I gave my all and still came up short, it would be too painful, so I gave 70 to 80 percent but no more. I really don't know why I made those choices then, but I do know that apathy is no longer acceptable to me—particularly spiritual apathy. When I awoke to the fact that my life involved more than me and mine, I began to push and strain against all my former limitations.

To arise a lioness, you must do the same. You may fail at your first attempts to develop strength, but that is also part of the learning process. I don't know of anyone who performs a feat perfectly the first time.

Second Peter 3:1, 7 says:

Hold your minds in a state of undistracted attention....

God is poised, ready to speak his word again, ready to give the signal.

Notice *you* are in charge of holding your mind at attention. Each and every day you have the power to choose whether to be attentive and focused or dull and distracted. It is high-alert time, because our God is poised. He is in position to make right what is wrong in this world. He is primed and ready and assured of victory. When our God Most High gives the signal, will you, like the lioness, be strong, limber, and ready to pounce?

Allow the Holy Spirit to assess your strength in the light of God's Word, and allow hardship to become a training session, knowing you might rise up from it invincible. Allow the weight of God's Word and the tempering and training of the Holy Spirit to quicken and develop the weak or injured areas of your life. Shift your focus from how you look in your clothing to who you are in your spirit. Above all, do not fear your strength. Like the lioness, glorify God with it. Remember, when all the earth is filled with fear and is wondering what is going on, the God of heaven and earth, the Creator of all, calls you to display his fearsome wonder in how you portray your life.

Do you believe that? What is it about you that inspires wonder? Can you "hear" with your heart? Do you know how to strategize? Are you skilled or creative? Are you a mother or teacher? Can you plan a seminar or family reunion? Can you transform a room from disorganized and cluttered to beautiful? Or are you a page, waiting to be written?

None of us will truly find fulfillment until we realize our place as one who lends strength to many. Lovely lioness sister, we need your fearless strength. It is indeed wonderfully beautiful.

5

Strength Is for Service

Each one of us needs to look after the good of the people around us, asking ourselves, "How can I help?"

ROMANS 15:2

There is a fierce serenity in the world of the lioness that we rarely observe unless we are out in the wild. I was reminded of this when I viewed the documentary featuring the introduction and resettling of predatory cats into a region of South Africa. At the beginning of the program, the commentator loosely narrated the story of two groups of lions as they were being introduced into a reserve park. The first group consisted of two young lionesses and one young lion.

The three lions had been living in a small, enclosed area that was temporarily attached to the extensive perimeter of an electric fence bordering the reserve. The wardens had rolled back a portion of the fence, which opened up to the lions a vast, unfamiliar, and unexplored expanse of land. Daunted by the sudden opening, the trio of lions were unsure how to respond.

The wardens had anticipated this reaction and devised a strategy for how they might motivate the young lions to cross into the newly opened territory. They decided not to feed the lions for several days in order for their appetites to lure them out of their confinement and into their new home with the promise of a fresh kill.

I watched with interest as the park rangers off-loaded the carcass of a large buck from the back of their truck and placed it outside the small enclosure but well within the borders of the lions' new home. The lions watched intently and lifted their heads when they smelled the buck's scent.

Even though these young lions were hungry, they were also cautious. The male lion would not budge from his place of safety in the African brush. As he watched, the two lionesses approached the opening in the fence, crossing paths as they paced distrustfully back and forth. It was as if they were reconstructing the limits where the electric fence had once stood. Together they sniffed the air, sniffed the ground, and then retreated behind a section of the fence, only to return and pause before the opening. It seemed as if they were trying to work out what had happened. Why was this opening suddenly before them? Was it a trick?

Finally one of the lionesses decided to go for it. Her hunger won out over her hesitation. She boldly crossed the line and approached the slain buck. At the halfway point she glanced back to her sister, as though inviting her to join her on the other side of the fence. The second lioness remained poised on the threshold a moment longer and then caught up with her sister. Together the two of them circled and sniffed the buck, making certain all was well. But the lion remained behind. As he watched, the lionesses took a tentative taste.

The kill was good, the meat fresh, but rather than dive into their feast, they did a curious thing. The lionesses grabbed hold of the buck by the neck and a leg, and the two of them dragged the carcass back into the enclosure so the lion could eat his share alongside them. Their actions gave me pause. I was impressed by their inclusion of the hesitant lion. I loved that they were not willing to feast without him.

It's beautiful when women know how to do this.

Helping Those Who Falter

Will we allow the noble example of our sister lionesses to speak to us and inspire our actions, interactions, and responses? Will we be the type of women who will take the time and make the effort to bring back the goodness we find in the newly opened expanses God is setting before his daughters?

Yes, I understand that turning back or waiting for others slows you down, but only at first. The deliberate extension of goodness, generosity, and wisdom always wins out in the end. Whenever God begins to breathe new life and freedom into his people, some of us embrace it with joy and expectancy. Others hesitate, waiting to see what will happen. And still others resist it.

It is my hope and prayer that all of God's daughters will rise up and enter into the freedom and purpose he is placing before us. And that those who are stronger, freer, or more established in truth will turn back and encourage onward those who are paused on the threshold.

I love how this is expressed in Romans 15.

Those of us who are strong and able in the faith need to step in and lend a hand to those who falter, and not just do what is most convenient for us. *Strength is for service, not status.* (verses 1–2)

The strong and able are charged to step in and assist those who falter, to lend a hand to those who pause, hesitate, waver, or weaken in their resolve. I love watching this dynamic unfold. There are so many women, young and old, who feel there is something larger inside them. They want to move forward and invade the space that now surrounds them. They stand on the threshold, looking toward the wild that God is calling them into, yet they hesitate.

Not long ago a lovely, earnest young girl approached me after a meeting. The God-dream within her was so large that our chance encounter did not give her the space or time to share all she wrestled to express. So she went home and with great care wrote an e-mail of epic proportions that expressed all she was feeling and sent it to me. Afterward she felt embarrassed, but she didn't need to be. As I read her words, I understood her angst. I was stunned by how much her words echoed my own feelings when I have gone through a similar season of transition, and I told her as much.

Often it is enough to know that others have crossed the bridge before us and found their way safely to the other side. Sometimes those who falter simply need a glance back from a sister who is already safely there. The look back is enough to communicate, "Hey, sister! I am out here, and not only is it all clear…it is all good!"

LIFTING RELIGION'S WEIGHT

Other women falter by staggering. Even though more and more women are discovering the freedom God has for them, some still stumble under the weight of religion. Only in the last decade have women been invited to speak to mixed-gender crowds. Many women and churches still struggle to accept this freedom. This was certainly true for me.

I was fearless when speaking to God's daughters, but add some guys into the mix, and I began to sweat—literally. Nervous and afraid of making a mistake, I tripped all over myself until one morning when both the pastor hosting me and one of my fearless girlfriends asked me to knock it off. "Why don't you act the same way in front of the men as you do in front of the women?" they challenged.

I answered truthfully, "I honestly don't know…"

"Well, can you hurry up and figure it out? We need you to stop being so hesitant!"

Their words hit me. I believe that in order for churches to be healthy, they need the voice of both genders. My hesitancy was actually undermining this belief! I was not lifting my voice in strength. In fact, I was almost apologetic in front of the men—not concerning the Scriptures but concerning my gender. Once my reluctance was pointed out to me, I began to push through it.

I still prefer to talk to women, but I no longer apologize if I am asked to minister to men. In my experience, if a man asks you to speak, then he wants you to give it your all. You know you are with true friends when they lift, encourage, correct, and then spur you on. Sadly, far too often the opposite is true.

Instead of giving you God's Law as food and drink by which you can banquet on God, they package it in bundles of rules, loading you down like pack animals. They seem to take pleasure in watching you stagger under these loads, and wouldn't think of lifting a finger to help. (Matthew 23:4)

The religious leaders of Jesus's day enjoyed it when they saw others laboring under rules. Why do you think they felt this way? My guess is that they felt lifted or superior when they saw others struggling under the laws they had created. It made them feel smug and somehow closer to God.

The above passage makes an important point. God's law was supposed to be a banquet, not a burden. Food gives strength, but labor drains it. We are called to represent God—what he is doing and all he offers—as a feast for everyone to partake in. We are to serve others from the abundance of God's goodness. This will at times require us to get rid of some of the religious baggage that has been loaded on God's sons and daughters.

Perhaps you are thinking, *You mean I can minister even if I am a single man or woman?* Yes! Let's throw away that hanging bag that says you have to be married to minister in the body of Christ. Paul wasn't married. Let's unpack the suitcase that says women can be trusted to work with children but not with adults. (Shouldn't we be more concerned about who works with our kids?) Can we also dump the steamer trunk that says we have to be perfect before we are in a position to speak God's promises? No one is perfect, and our insistence on this pretense is making the world around us nauseous. No more facades. Let's all admit our mistakes, learn from them, and move forward, lifting Jesus up.

Are we willing to use our freedom to lift the weight that religion has wrongly placed on others? Whenever God calls us to do something new—to cover new ground or tackle unfamiliar terrain—we are prone to trip and stumble. The church has made a lot of advances in the last ten years, and that is exciting, but not everyone is up to speed yet. Still, God is at work, opening previously closed doors and creating hunger in people's hearts so they might overcome their fears.

Recently I received an e-mail from a woman who three or four years ago had heard me teach that consecrated, anointed women could and should have a voice in the house of God. This concept initially alarmed her because it flew in the face of all she had known. She left confused and troubled by what I had said. Time passed, and as she studied and prayed, God began to confirm my teaching to her and to open up the very same door before her. At that point she realized that the conflict she had felt when she heard me speak was from God. Her discomfort was a result of his speaking to her about this issue. The words I had spoken years before had acted as seed in this woman's life that only now were springing into a harvest.

We are charged to speak the truth in love and to live in such a way that it invites others to journey with us. We are not to leave the weak and hungry in our wake.

Ezekiel 19:2 poses this question: "What is your mother? A lioness among lions!" (NLT).

When I first read this, I thought, *What does this mean?* To gain insight, I reviewed the context of Ezekiel 19. It paints a picture of a lioness raising two young cubs to become strong and mighty lions. I thought, *I want to learn to be a lioness among lions!* Who doesn't want to be the type of woman whose life and choices have the power to rear strong daughters and sons? I am honored to be welcomed into the world of so many women, but I want to be an asset to the men I do life with as well. I want to lift *all* who are fearful, weak, or struggling. And do you know what? You do as well. God has woven into the fabric of his daughters the desire to raise others.

HOPE TO THE HOPELESS

Sometimes lending a hand to the faltering is as simple as introducing hope. On a recent trip to Cambodia with Life Outreach, I roamed the streets at night, striking up conversations with girls trapped in prostitution. Whenever I approached these night-roaming daughters, they were guarded and almost mocking in their interactions with me. This pattern of disdain was replayed whether I approached an individual girl or a group of them. They met my questions with one-word answers and smirked among themselves. I am sure they wondered why a white, middle-aged American woman was addressing them. But as the conversation progressed, I would ask them about their dreams.

"What do you want for your life? If you could be or do anything, what would that look like?"

Without fail, I saw their faces transform at the invitation to dream and to hope their lives might be something more. In the midst of a nightmare, was someone actually asking them to dream? Suddenly I had answers as fast as my interpreter could relay them to me.

"I want to do hair!"

"I want to own a restaurant."

"I want to have my own stall in the marketplace where I sell beautiful things."

"I want to do any type of work where people will no longer look down on me."

"I want to make enough money to send some home to my family."

The girls couldn't stop talking. They shed their seductive poses and for a few, brief minutes looked like the young teenage girls they were.

These girls knew what they wanted, if only their cage had an open door! Whenever possible, we offered to help them escape their prison, and a few accepted our offer of help. But only those who could move beyond their shame were able to move forward. Guilt and shame held many of these girls just as captive as did their pimps.

In desperate situations like this, dreaming and knowing what you want is not enough. In most cases someone so trapped, so defeated, will hide within the enclosure, even when the door is thrown wide open. So in addition to offering to help these girls find a way out of prostitution, we brought goodness into their enclosure. We introduced them to Jesus. We told them that he was on their side and that he alone is the ultimate hope to the hopeless.

Whether they would invite him into their hearts and lives was up to them. You and I can walk alongside others and encourage them to move forward, but inevitably the final choice is theirs.

A Lioness Truth

Let's return for a moment to the lionesses in the documentary I mentioned at the beginning of this chapter. Why did they bring the carcass back for the lion to eat? Certainly they had other options. It was awkward dragging that large buck back into the enclosure so the lion could join in their feast. A more convenient option would have been for them to eat their fill, then leave the remains for the lion whenever he decided to come out on his own. Or they could have eaten their fill and then brought him the leftovers. It would have been much easier to transport part of a buck than the entire carcass. Their behavior seems the opposite of what we would expect, given the jungle law. If the animal kingdom is based on survival, why were these lionesses so generous? After all, sharing with a hungry lion meant less food for them.

Perhaps these lionesses knew something we have forgotten. Though they were young and immature, they instinctively understood that their future and the survival of their children was intimately tied to how they related to the lion. They chose to behave in a manner that would be remembered by the lion in his future season of strength. They honored the mighty lion that he would one day become, and they overlooked his current posture of cowering in the bush. The day would come when he would be fully grown and unafraid. He would remember that the lionesses had brought him food when he was young and too frightened to claim what was his own. On that day he would know he could trust and build a life with them. The instincts of the lionesses would sustain the pride and win his affection.

How many of us share this attitude?

Better yet, do *I* share their attitude?

Or have we adopted a less noble survival stance? Is our attitude, "Hey, too bad for you back there. I have a good thing going for me out here. God is preparing a feast for his daughters. If you're not willing to join us, stay in your enclosure and be that way!"?

We would be wise to learn the truth: *taking less now does not mean having less in our future.* Acts of honor are never lost in translation.

Strength is given us for service, not to convey status (see Romans 15:2). I wonder how much trouble would be averted in the world at large if everyone knew and adhered to this principle. What if we knew that our strength was to serve the weak, fearful, or timid? It would all be good! I believe at the end of this life, we all want to hear Jesus say, "Well done, good and faithful servant."

RISE UP FOR EXCELLENT SERVICE

This word *service* has multiple applications. It is both a verb and a noun. As a verb, it means "to repair, check, tune, and examine." Jesus did us a great "service" through his sacrifice and made us fit to stand before a holy God. We live in a way that reflects this life-giving service. He was broken so we might be repaired. The noun form of *service* can mean "ceremony, ritual, or sacrament." Sometimes I fear we've forgotten that the purpose of a church *service* is to learn how to serve God and one another well. Far too many Christians gather with the wrong expectation. They come to hear how God will serve them. Instead, let's come together for the purpose of reaching out to those who falter within our buildings and outside our sanctuaries.

With the promise of freedom, favor, and new opportunities opening up before us, let's move forward in the things of God so that none might fall behind. I love this charge:

> Don't imagine us leaders to be something we aren't. We are servants
> of Christ, not his masters. We are guides into God's most sublime
> secrets, not security guards posted to protect them. The requirements
> for a good guide are reliability and accurate knowledge. (1 Corinthi-
> ans 4:1–2)

We are to be guides, not security guards. We are to invite others into the kingdom, not keep them outside the mystery of God. We are charged to be reliable guides with accurate knowledge. Let's be certain to pause at the openings God has made for us and if necessary reach back so that others do not fall behind.

As a daughter of the Most High, your reach should be both generous and noble. The life of God liberates, while the law burdens. You have been released from the "eye for an eye and a tooth for a tooth" approach to Christianity. Yet there are far too many partially blind and toothless ones walking around in the body of Christ.

Never forget who you are—strong, majestic, fearless, fierce, protective, at rest, and unworried. God repeatedly compared the strength of his royal children to lions and lionesses.

> Like a lion, Israel crouches and lies down;
> like a lioness, who dares to arouse her? (Numbers 24:9, NLT)

If you forget your fierce and fearless nature, then all who look to you for protection and guidance will be at risk. The body of Christ is made up of noble, powerful guardians who have awakened to the realization that God has opened up a wide expanse before us.

Dear sisters, lionesses, and friends…

I can't tell you how much I long for you to enter this wide-open, spacious life. We didn't fence you in. The smallness you feel comes from within you. Your lives aren't small, but you're living them in a small way. I'm speaking as plainly as I can and with great affection. Open up your lives. Live openly and expansively! (2 Corinthians 6:11–13)

Do you hear this? We have been invited to enter into the wild, wide-open spaces of God. This is a summons to live expansively, here and now. You don't have to wait until heaven to see heaven's power released on earth. God is not the one fencing you in.

But the lionesses did not move outside their enclosure until their hunger exceeded their desire to be safe. In the same way, our lack of vision or hunger for something more can limit and restrain us from stepping out into the wild. We are emboldened or held captive by how we see ourselves, our world, and our God. The world "out there" can look daunting if you imagine it a dark, scary place.

Open your eyes and remember who you are—a golden bearer of light who has the power to dispel darkness wherever she goes. *"The Spirit in you is far stronger than anything in the world"* (1 John 4:4). It is not even a close match. The Spirit within you *far exceeds* the might of any opposition you may encounter in this world! It is the Most High God who calls you out. He sent his Son to die on a cross so you might cross over from death to life and from this world's places of confinement into the eternal expanse. Even before you drew your first breath, he had made a way to release you from captivity. He chose to confine himself and experience our small, fenced-in life so you could join him in the vast freedom of the kingdom.

Even now he calls to each of us, "Cross over and enter in!"

6

Under the Same Mission

Every time we liberate a woman, we liberate a man.
Margaret Mead

In the lion world, there is no gender confusion. Lions are not trying to be lionesses, and lionesses are not trying to be lions. Neither gender copies or competes for the role of the other. Both are comfortable in their skin and celebrate the unique strengths of their respective gender. In addition to male and female, within the pride there is the alpha or lead lion and the alpha or lead lioness, but the exercising of this status usually comes into play at mealtime.

Lions are the only members of the cat family to exhibit a notable and immediately visible difference between the sexes. The term used to describe this diversity is sexual dimorphism. Simply put, there is more than one indicator of their gender.

Lions have a large mane encircling their necks and framing their faces. This mane highlights the distinct and specialized role the lead lion plays in the pride and makes the lion look intimidating on the African plain. The lioness's lack of a mane gives her seamless coloring so she can stalk her prey virtually unseen. Without the additional weight of a mane, she is able to keep pace and sustain a charge for longer distances.

Healthy lions and lionesses know they need one another. They would never dream of doing life without one another. In their world one strength is no less important than the other. The lion protects; the lioness provides. This crucial balance means healthy, strong alpha male lions wouldn't attempt life without the aid of a company of powerful lionesses. In the lions' world, the males battle to win a gathering of lionesses and therefore access to their realm. Why is this? The related lionesses, not the lions, control the land. The coalition of male lions who lead the pride changes every two to three years, but the lionesses remain.

The alpha lion knows that if he wants to flourish (not merely exist) he must establish himself in the eyes of the lionesses with strength. Then to have his progeny hold the pride area, he must have the help of strong, capable lionesses. He doesn't surround himself with the weak and passive in the hope of coercing them into submission. He looks for a highly specialized cooperative unit of lionesses.

He welcomes their strength and purposely chooses those who've proven their skill and stamina to hunt and sustain their young and therefore maintain and expand their territory. He looks for those who exhibit strength, knowing they will ultimately make better providers for the entire pride and capable mothers to train his young. (Not that male lions are particularly nurturing; they're not.) As an added benefit, healthy, strong lionesses are willing to breed more often, which gives him the chance to mate and establish a stronger lineage.

The lioness will not reproduce if she fears that she cannot provide for her cubs or that they will be poorly protected. Because of this, the lioness is drawn to strong alpha lions rather than to the weaker ones. The lead lion or lions (often it is a group of related brothers) must earn the right to enjoy the provision, strength, and nurture lionesses bring to the pride. This privilege is won by an open show of strength between the lion groups.

The contest ends when the weaker lions are run off by the stronger. Sometimes the alpha lion kills his challenger. If the weaker lion survives, he is exiled and forced out of the pride's territory, which means the loss of prime hunting. He will either move on and look for a pride of lionesses elsewhere, or he'll be reduced to scavenging.

The lionesses watch on the sidelines. They want the most powerful lion to father their young and protect their pride from attacks and harassment. They've been known to pit lions against each other to ensure that the mightiest wins, and then they accept the victor. By winning his territory, the lion proves his genetic pool worthy and more likely to survive the rigors of the wild.

Once dominance is determined, the loyalty of the lionesses is won. Any remaining males in the pride may be driven off. The alpha lion is willing to forgo their company, but there is no way he will give up his girls. It is not just because he wants them around for breeding. They are the providers of food and community. The stronger and more stunning his group of lionesses, the more powerful and secure the lion, magnificent king of the beasts.

There is no need to dominate when those around you know you would do everything in your power to protect them. The lion's might means safety for both the lionesses and their young. Only those who are unsure of their power try to dominate.

Once established, the mighty lion does not feel the need to oppress the lionesses to showcase his power. What does he have to prove? He has won. Who outranks him? Likewise, our King—our Lion of Judah—doesn't dominate; he elevates.

UNDER THE SAME MISSION

The lion invites the lioness to rest in the shadow of his protection, and she invites him to feast on the goodness and promise she brings. He protects her life, and she in turn gives him legacy.

Consider the word *submission* for a moment. What comes to mind? Probably Ephesians 5:22, about wives submitting to their husbands. Interestingly, many Christians have taken this verse and created an extreme and limiting definition for the word. I believe the word *submission* has been distorted beyond God's intent for it. Many Christian women have believed their primary value lies in their ability to serve men. They have not realized that speaking in the church, respectfully voicing their opinions, or taking on the responsibility of a leadership role *is serving*.

I heard a definition of *submission* that framed and aligned it with God's plan for all Christians, not just couples. Consider this: the prefix *sub* means "under," and *mission* is an assignment. Put them together, and we can draw a conclusion that *submission* means "under the same assignment or mission." Personally, John and I are under the same mission. We are committed to raising godly children and building a healthy, vibrant marriage. In the realm of the church, our mission is to undergird pastors and strengthen individuals.

But think about it. Aren't we all ministers of reconciliation—God's ambassadors to the lost? The following two verses capture our mission as God's male and female ambassadors:

God put the world square with himself through the Messiah, giving the world a fresh start by offering forgiveness of sins. God has given us the task of telling everyone what he is doing. We're Christ's representatives. *God uses us to persuade men and women to drop their differences and enter into God's work of making things right between them.* (2 Corinthians 5:19–20)

Bottom line: they will know our Jesus is real when we love and work well with one another. This should be the joint goal of all men and women, whether single or married, leader or lay person. The force of the Fall is over. God's forgiveness is freely offered to all. There is no need to lay blame if his sacrifice has rendered us all blameless. God wants us all—male and female—to tell everyone what *he is doing*! Instead, we have been too busy telling each other what we can or cannot do.

He wants us to work together as persuasive influencers who encourage and convince men and women to drop their conflicts (whatever they might be) and enter into his work. This issue of conflict resolution should apply to every area of human relationships and interactions. This charge is not just a gender issue; it is a race, socioeconomic, family, church, and marketplace dynamic as well. He wants reconciliation for all of us!

Now we look inside, and what we see is that anyone united with the Messiah gets a fresh start, is created new. The old life is gone; a new life burgeons! Look at it! All this comes from the God who settled the relationship between us and him, and then called us to settle our relationships with each other. (2 Corinthians 5:17–18)

"Anyone" means, well, *any one*. Any man, any woman, any child united to Christ is re-created. The old life disappears. The word *burgeons* in the verse above is a verb meaning "to mushroom." This is an interesting choice of words because mushrooms explode with growth—they multiply, prosper, grow rapidly, and flourish in places where there was nothing but decay before. Our new life in Christ is more than a replacement concept. It is life multiplied within, and it is available to everyone.

Lions and lionesses have already settled their relationships with each other. Lionesses understand they are under the same mission as the lion. What is their mission? Their mission is to establish a generation of lions with legacy and strength. To accomplish this, they raise, protect, and provide for their young well. Both lion and lioness have a role to play within that mission, and neither cat usurps the role of the other.

I have seen what should be natural order taken to two opposing extremes. On one end of the spectrum, women have been suppressed in the name of submission. At the other end, some women have elevated their femininity to the level of divinity. More on this a bit later. First I want to share an example of the distortion of submission.

TWITTER TWIST

You have likely heard of or participated in the abbreviated form of electronic communication called Twitter. It is good for snippets of information and at best provides mere windows into issues of life and thought.

One day I posted a concept I'd addressed in detail in my book *Fight Like a Girl*. It was a quote on leadership: "Gender alone does not qualify a man to lead, just as gender alone should not disqualify a woman.[1] Virtue qualifies both male and female." Please note, I did not restrict it to church leadership or confine it to marriage. I simply stated that virtue was a necessary quality for leaders, whether they were male or female.

I put it out there on Twitter, which posted it to my Facebook page. Then I went about my day. I didn't think what I said was controversial. I felt it was a given. I had no idea what kind of fallout would follow my statement.

When I received more than one hundred responses, I knew I'd hit a nerve. While I'd been busy with daily activities, a debate had arisen on Facebook. A few Christian women were incensed.

"How dare you say a wife could lead her husband if she deemed herself more virtuous!" wrote one woman.

Okay… Is that what I'd said?

Others accused me of tossing out the scriptures that said only a man could be a church elder. Had I mentioned church eldership? Then there was a discussion about leadership in general. Some women explained to the Facebook audience that a woman was *never* supposed to be a leader.

A sincere young girl looking for clarity raised the question, "Are you saying a senior pastor's wife is not a leader?" The reply was a resounding, "No, she is not a leader! She has the honor of supporting her husband."

Now I was confused! As opinions flew, the dialogue turned into a discussion on submission. Some argued I was a leader; others said I was not, simply because I was a woman. Then allowances were made for me because I was submitted to my husband and therefore was a leader under him.

Let's pause and reason together. Why is it that whenever a gender discussion comes up, it seems to mire down into an issue of women's submission to men? If I am a leader, it is because God has made me one. Quite simply, leaders have people following them. Some of us are leaders, whether we ever signed up to be one or not. So God help us all to lead by example. To address the confusion, let's read Paul's leadership charge to Timothy.

A leader must be well-thought-of, committed to his wife, cool and collected, accessible, and hospitable. He must know what he's talking about, not be overfond of wine, not pushy but gentle, not thin-skinned, not money-hungry. He must handle his own affairs well, attentive to his own children and having their respect. For if some-one is unable to handle his own affairs, how can he take care of God's church? He must not be a new believer, lest the position go to his head and the Devil trip him up. Outsiders must think well of him, or else the Devil will figure out a way to lure him into his trap.

The same goes for those who want to be servants in the church: serious, not deceitful, not too free with the bottle, not in it for what they can get out of it. They must be reverent before the mystery of the faith, not using their position to try to run things. Let them prove themselves first. If they show they can do it, take them on. (1 Timothy 3:2–10)

In the verses above, Paul is listing the qualifications for male leadership. Then he goes on to say:

No exceptions are to be made for women—*same qualifications:* seri-ous, dependable, not sharp-tongued, not overfond of wine. Servants in the church are to be committed to their spouses, attentive to their own children, and diligent in looking after their own affairs. Those who do this servant work will come to be highly respected, a real credit to this Jesus-faith. (1 Timothy 3:11–13)

Why would Paul give a list of leadership qualifications for women if their gender alone disqualified them? When John and I are hiring for a position at our ministry office, we give a list of qualifications. If applicants are unqualified, we don't hire them. It matters not if they are male or female. Paul didn't say that if a leader is not a male, don't entrust him. He said, male or female, if they do not meet the qualifications, don't appoint them. Paul's emphasis was on a list of qualifications. Paul said no exceptions were to be made for the women; they would have to model the same standards. You may ask what about the charge that the elder is to be the husband of one wife? Well, women didn't marry multiple husbands, so that directive was exclusive to men.

In 1 Timothy 3:11–13, Paul instructed Timothy in the qualifications of women in leadership and then he went on to break it down for women servants or deacons in the church. How do I know this? Let's read verses 1–2 and see what was said before the detailed description was given for the men.

If *anyone* wants to provide leadership in the church, good! But there are preconditions. (1 Timothy 3:1–2)

Notice the word "anyone"? Likewise, the English Standard Version says "anyone," and the New Living Translation says "someone."

Why is it women can be leaders everywhere but in the church? If God had no problem empowering women before and after the Fall, why are we reticent to empower them after redemption?

At one point the Facebook debate among women got so intense that a man stepped in and asked, "Why are you women arguing against yourselves? We need your contribution, but you are stopping each other!" There is a lot of truth in what he said. We frequently stop or minimize one another. Instead of supporting and encouraging one another for the cause of Christ, we perpetuate an oppression that renders us ineffective to be all we're supposed to be as women and as Christians.

This unexpected social-networking incident reminded me of the need for gender issues to be addressed not only in the family but also in the church. The world we live in needs to see the true heart of God and his original intent modeled in every aspect of the lives and leadership of God's sons and daughters.

SEXIST ATTITUDES

I would love to think it's no longer necessary to address sexist attitudes in the American church. Yes, I am intentionally singling out my nation. As I travel and have the opportunity to gather more of a worldview, I see that our traditional lack of female involvement doesn't work in other places on the globe. In some nations there would be no church if not for the contribution of women.

> *Everything* God created *is good,* and *to be received* with *thanks.* Nothing is to be sneered at and thrown out. God's Word and our prayers make every item in creation holy. (1 Timothy 4:4–5)

If every *thing* God created is good and to be received, accepted, and given welcome with gratitude, how much more should *people* be received in this manner? Men and women are *good.*

If something is God created, then we're charged not to sneer at it or throw it out. To *sneer* means to scorn, mock, turn your nose up at, or laugh at. All these actions devalue an item, person, or their role and contribution.

The word *throw* appears self-explanatory, but let's look at one of its finer points. Along with toss, hurl, and fling away, to *throw* can mean to confuse, bewilder, complicate, or perplex a matter. Add the word *out,* which can mean to make absent, and you have a picture of *rejection.* I am afraid this is what happens all too frequently to women in the church. They are tossed aside without welcome, so their voices, value, and contributions are absent. And *both* genders allow it in the name of submission.

Consequently, both men and women suffer extensive loss of value. Obviously, men are received into higher leadership positions in the church more often than women are, but sometimes they are crippled by a lack of women's insight. But are we thankful for the men? Do we see them as God sees them—as good?

Or do we sneer at their behavior? I'm not talking about laughing together. It is impossible not to laugh at the hilarity of humans. Just our existence declares God's extensive sense of humor. Here I am warning about mocking and depreciating the genders. I bet it happens more than you know. Our entertainment industry regularly dishonors men and sexualizes women.

We have allowed sexist attitudes to take us to a place where women who feel devalued resent men. So where do we go from here? Unfortunately, in response some women have moved toward an appalling extreme.

THE FEMININE DIVINE

As I wrote this book, I happened to notice on Amazon two other titles that flanked one of my previous books. Both were authored by advocates of "feminine divine" theology—a belief in female deities or a self-actualizing goddess. I heard God whisper, *Buy the book on the right and on the left of yours, and find out how we lost their voices.*

As I turned the pages and read the entries and questions, I heard anguish and heartbreak. These were two powerful and influential women who had been profoundly wounded and disappointed by the church. I felt like weeping for the loss of their brilliance.

Why did they feel they had no choice but to erect goddess worship outside the house of God?

Were their questions so sharp or pointed that they challenged the status quo? Was their intelligence so bright they intimidated church leaders? Had their voices been squelched in church because of an exaggerated definition of submission or a diminished representation of redemption?

I have no doubt these women frightened both men and women with their questions.

Perhaps you've never experienced the search and disappointment they had, but I certainly have. I know I am not alone. I receive letters, e-mails, and questions that repeat the theme "Tell me again why I have value as a daughter of the Most High."

The following is a telling excerpt from Sue Monk Kidd's book *The Dance of the Dissident Daughter.* In her own words, she opens a window to a common experience of the evangelical church daughter.

"Woman was the first to sin and the second to be created," he said.
Then he went on to talk about Eve, how she was created for man's
benefit, that she was unworthy because she disobeyed God and
offered Adam the forbidden fruit....

My heart sank. If I could have put the feeling into words, I would have said, "God, how *could* you?"[2]

The author goes on to share how she had a hard time reconciling her perception of God with the viewpoint of the church. I agree. God would never make such a sweeping, hopeless generalization about any of us—male or female.

If we say women should have no opportunity for leadership because Eve and her daughters are easily deceived, then we must slam the door in the face of Adam and his sons. He *knowingly* sinned and betrayed God's entrustment.

The contrast of Adam's and Eve's infractions could be likened to the difference between a crime of passion and premeditated murder. Eve was caught off guard; Adam knew full well what hung in the balance.

If you sin without knowing what you're doing, God takes that into account. But if you sin knowing full well what you're doing, that's a different story entirely. (Romans 2:12)

What sort of religious world have we fashioned for ourselves when intelligent female searchers of truth cannot find answers within our gates? If we do not step up to the plate and find some answers, what will happen to our daughters if they dare to raise such questions?

And God help the men if we continue on this course! Men do not grow healthy and strong through the silence of women. Men grow stronger by the addition of our voices because the challenge of a daughter's questions serves to raise men higher, which makes them freer. The perspective of women tempers and refines men, just as they create an environment for the women to flourish.

As I read the essays of the authors of the feminine divine philosophy, not one inquiry caught me off guard. It was the empty answers they received that broke my heart.

I feel as though a sea of women's tears separates us. I see them on the distant shore, and I'm saddened. These women call themselves dissidents and goddesses, but I would rather call them friends and daughters of the Most High. Their accusations yet ring loudly in my ears, for I found more truth in their complaints than in the answers they were given.

On the poignant pages I read many stories of sadness. One was captured in the account of an ob-gyn who repeatedly witnessed American mothers apologizing to their husbands when their labor brought forth a daughter. As a mother of four sons, this idea is almost unfathomable. I enjoy the treasure of a husband who loves women. Though he celebrated the birth of each of our sons, he hoped for a daughter. When I repeated these stories to him, he was shocked. If we had ever welcomed a daughter into our world, we would have declared her lovely and longed for!

Finding no answers, value, or room for contribution within the walls of religion, these daughters established a realm of worship outside of what they saw as patriarchal tyranny. In woods and beaches they moved to what they perceived to be a kinder, gentler realm of queen divine.

Breathe! I am not advocating we follow their course. I choose neither their queen nor the angry king of religion. I choose our Creator, the God Most High.

A QUEST FOR DIVINE PURPOSE

Listen to this desperate invitation from feminine divine leader Marianne Williamson in her book *A Woman's Worth*:

When I say, "Go talk to Mary," I *mean* "Go talk to Mary"—as in, go to a church, light a candle, sit in a pew, and let yourself become very serious about this. Tell her, "Mary, I wish to know who I am as a wife or girlfriend or mother or daughter. I wish to be the woman I am capable of being. I wish to have your purity and clarity and level of enlightenment. May the essence of my womanhood become more radiant than my external self."[3]

It is not wrong to pray and ask to be the woman you are capable of being. The issue is to whom she suggests we direct our prayers. Williamson then made allowances for those uncomfortable with Catholicism.

If Mary doesn't feel comfortable for you, that's OK too. Find a Greek goddess or a female Indian avatar you can relate to, or any other symbol of feminine divinity, and begin a relationship with her.[4]

A relationship with her? Immediately after this suggestion she shared the reason for her anger.

The world as it is has very little use for your womanhood. You are considered a weaker sex and are treated as a sexual object. You are thoroughly dispensable except for bearing children. Your youth is the measure of your worth, and your age is the measure of your worthlessness. Do not look to the world for your sustenance or for your identity as a woman because you will not find them there. The world despises you. God adores you.[5]

I am so thankful she ends with the truth that God adores you. But there is no mistaking her pain. She grasps for a real feminine divine connection. Here she goes so far as to suggest a Greek goddess, hoping that by appealing to an image of divine, enduring feminine beauty and power, she will recapture what is so desperately missing in our own connections. I pray she finds the truth she seeks.

As a former Catholic, I understand her suggestion. I am not advocating Mary-worship on any level, but with the Protestant removal of Mary as a deity (which she is not!), they effectively removed her as an example for women.

Mary is not a god, but she was godly. She is not a statue to light votive candles to, but she was a woman whose example lights our way. She foreshadowed what was to come—daughters who would partner with God and reveal Jesus.

Did I say Jesus? Interesting point. I searched the pages of *A Woman's Worth* and found almost no mention of Jesus, Mary's son. How can Mary be valid without Jesus? So what is the real invitation here?

It is not literally about Mary, Athena, or Aphrodite. It is about an unnamed spirit of our own making!

The feminine divine authors spoke of God and goddesses, religion and men, but rarely of the beautiful Savior, God's Son, Jesus the Christ. They talked about queens, enchantresses, and maternal turtles but no Son who rose from the dead. Why would mothers avoid the revelation of a son? Their words danced around Jesus, even borrowed his words, but failed to mention his name.

Then again, this is no surprise. If I can elevate myself to the divine, why would I need a savior?

The position of goddess is not simply one of power; it begs worship. But we must not worship man, woman, or creation. We are to worship God alone. There is no need to create a female deity that adds value to women if the church would preach truth and original intent.

The God of heaven and earth, the Lord Most High, openly declared the value of women in his redemptive plan. God brought forth his Son without the seed of man. Joseph was charged to protect Mary and the holy child she carried. God's Spirit quickened life in the virgin womb of a young, slightly frightened Hebrew girl. She was not chanting and calling herself a goddess. Mary was willing—and even doubting—if she was able! May we echo her words and make them our own. *Be unto us, heavenly Father, according to your promises; we believe that what you said you would do, you will do. Lift the oppressed of earth, and reveal your Son through our lives.*

Our quest for divine purpose will not be found in elevating ourselves above men in an attempt to realize the goddess within. Men have not found true strength or freedom by dominating women. And women are not effective when they allow their strength to be usurped by excessive doctrines. Both genders are allies and guardians, not enemies and gods.

The desire to be worshiped is a test for every one of us. It is the very one Lucifer failed. The desire for power is not ungodly; we each (male and female) steward a measure of faith, power, and influence.

Humans were never created for absolute power. It is a draft or role too difficult for angels to handle, and Jesus, the very Son of God, did not dare to grasp equality with God. In Paul's letter to the Philippians, we are charged not to follow this gentile power positioning.

> Think of yourselves the way Christ Jesus thought of himself. He had
> equal status with God but didn't think so much of himself that he
> had to cling to the advantages of that status no matter what. Not at

all. When the time came, he set aside the privileges of deity and took on the status of a slave, became *human*! Having become human, he stayed human. It was an incredibly humbling process. He didn't claim special privileges. Instead, he lived a selfless, obedient life and then died a selfless, obedient death—and the worst kind of death at that: a crucifixion.

Because of that obedience, God lifted him high and honored him far beyond anyone or anything, ever, so that all created beings in heaven and on earth—even those long ago dead and buried—will bow in worship before this Jesus Christ, and call out in praise that he is the Master of all, to the glorious honor of God the Father. (Philippians 2:5–11)

Our world needs servants. I can't imagine my Jesus—who stooped to lift everyone—being as demanding as some of us are. Sadly, I fear we have misrepresented our King. Why else would world leaders for peace be so justified in saying, "If it weren't for Christians, I'd be a Christian." And, "I like your Christ. I do not like your Christians. They are so unlike your Christ," as Mahatma Gandhi said.[6]

Do you hear a cry and the desperate need for you to rise up as a fearless seeker of truth? We are charged to love intentionally, to reach outside of our sterile barrenness to the lost and hurting.

If the church will not make room for you, take his love to the highways and byways. There are more than enough broken and hurting people outside our walls that would welcome your involvement. Reach out to your community, your homeless, your professions, your school system… Create a life so large and bright it is irresistible.

It is time to rise to a stature that people can look up to.

What do we do now? Do we continue to make issues out of what God has settled? Can we balance our thinking to avoid the extremes of submission and feminine divinity? Can we honor men? Let's follow the example of the lion and lioness and rise up together—with the men, not as subservient underlings nor as angry goddesses.

THE VALUE OF STRONG WOMEN

As I write, Twitter, post messages on Facebook, and stand before women, whether I am communicating in meetings or by way of broadcasts, I continually take every opportunity to proclaim the value of women. I deliberately remind them there is a need for their voice and contribution in the church, outside the church, and on local and worldwide levels. It is my prayer that they will not only believe and celebrate it but that they will live it.

After speaking, I consistently hear this question raised: "Can you please tell the men this?" Their suggestions come in whispers as though it might be dangerous if someone overheard and discovered they had dared to suggest I openly share such a thing.

I used to think it was enough to encourage only the women. There is incredible value in speaking to women in intimate, safe settings. But as this journey of God's daughters continues, I've learned that speaking this type of encouragement only to women is not enough, just as there is limited value when only one side of a coin is intact.

Over the last few years, my world enlarged, and my voice was invited and welcomed into the Sunday morning church world. This of course includes men. As I raise my voice in mixed-gender settings, I let them know that women are amazing.

Rarely do I see the men contest this. I intentionally let them know I think men are amazing too! In the last few years, I have seen a lot of tears from the men. I've watched as husbands and wives embraced and called off their wrestling matches. I love what happens as they ask for forgiveness from each other for their silly power struggles.

Dear lioness sister, men are not our problem. This issue runs much deeper. Satan is our enemy and a deceiver who strips both genders of their dignity. Though they aren't the problem, men can and should be a part of the answer. Something dynamic happens when men shoulder some of the load of the restoration of dignity and power alongside the women.

Sometimes positioning yourself to be heard is more than half the battle. The men in your world need to be able to hear you, and they need to hear others who are encouraging men and women to rise up together. If there is to be change, we must all be saying the same thing. Let's echo God's stance.

To do this, I want to take an in-depth look at 1 Corinthians 11. I am going to break it down into separate and distinct pieces, then cover the perspective of the whole.

Don't, by the way, read too much into the differences here between men and women. (verse 10)

Paul positioned all that will follow with the charge not to read too much into or make too big a deal of the difference between the sexes. Yes, there are differences, but these were never meant to divide us. They exist to unite us.

Neither man nor woman can go it alone or claim priority. (verse 11)

With this statement he declares the interdependence of the sexes; if there is mutual dependence, then there is no priority given to male or to female.

Man was created first, as a beautiful shining reflection of God—that is true. But the head on a woman's body clearly outshines in beauty the head of her "head," her husband. (verse 11)

Man is first created as a reflection of God—all true. Then here comes the "but." The woman's beauty outshines her husband. Note this specifically addresses husband and wife.

The first woman came from man, true—but ever since then, every man comes from a woman! (verse 12)

Again it's true the first woman, Eve, came from the man, Adam. Then Paul uses the word "but" again to balance the other side of the scale with "ever since" all men have come from women.

And since virtually everything comes from God anyway, let's quit going through these "who's first" routines. (verse 12)

Now that the scales are perfectly balanced, Paul rises above the back-and-forth gender debate and lends divine perspective: everything comes from God, so quit arguing about preeminence! This should settle a lot. God alone is first. He alone is holy, just, love, truth, the way, the life, the beginning, and the end.

Never imagine God is swayed by the legislation of our denominations. He is not impressed with our bylaws and what we allow and don't allow. God moves into action, and when he sees people rightly related and under his sway, it is there that he commands a blessing.

How wonderful, how beautiful,
  when brothers and sisters get along!
. . . .
Yes, that's where GOD commands the blessing,
  ordains eternal life. (Psalm 133:1, 3)

Throughout history the church has been divided on these matters, but I, for one, am not willing for that to remain our legacy. But what I think and feel is a small thing compared to God's decree of how it will be. Things will change.

"In the Last Days," God says,
"I will pour out my Spirit
  on every kind of people:
Your sons will prophesy,
  also your daughters;
Your young men will see visions,
  your old men dream dreams.
When the time comes,
  I'll pour out my Spirit
On those who serve me, men and women both,
  and they'll prophesy.
I'll set wonders in the sky above
  and signs on the earth below,
Blood and fire and billowing smoke." (Acts 2:17–19)

In the last days, God will have his say. This imagery of blood, fire, and billowing smoke sounds very much like the ancient altar of Hebrew sacrifice.

It was where the people gathered to bring what was acceptable to God Most High. Their offering was presented and translated by fire into the realm of heaven.

In this New Testament vision, there is no mention of rams, heifers, and oxen to be consumed on the altar. Instead, we see the lifted voices of sons and daughters, old and young, all insightful prophetic servants of the Most High. Our fire does not burn on the altar of worship. Our fire resides within as we are consumed and propelled by his Spirit.

In years past I might have been afraid to address gender issues so directly. But at this point in my life, I am willing to push the envelope if necessary. My husband does not fear my strength—he welcomes it. My sons are not attracted to images of weak, voiceless, suppressed women. But is it right for me to be so supported when others are not? Our world needs women who will give their voice on behalf of the oppressed everywhere. This means being at ease with all we were created to be alongside one another.

It's time for us to lay aside our gender issues and move away from extremes that render us ineffective. It's time to wake up to how God has purposed us to be—strong in him, an asset to men, and a voice of redemption to the lost and hurting in the world.

7

Greet and Groom

For attractive lips, speak words of kindness. For
lovely eyes, seek out the good in people. For a
slim figure, share your food with the hungry.
For beautiful hair, let a child run his or her
fingers through it once a day. For poise, walk
with the knowledge that you never walk alone.

SAM LEVENSON

When lionesses groom each other, it is all a part of their greeting. The
grooming begins when the lioness is a cub. Once a cub has been
spotted, there is no escape from the obligatory kisses of the lioness. No cub
is allowed to go unlicked. I imagine a scene something like this: After an
exciting time of observing the grown-up lions hunting for food, a cub re-
enters the intimacy of the pride. All of a sudden, the cub hesitates, thinking,
Oh no! Here she comes! My auntie is going to lick me and slather her saliva all

over my face! Sounds a lot like what happens when a niece or nephew walks into a room full of Italian aunts who have come to visit, doesn't it?

Cubs are not the only ones subjected to this intimate face-to-face greeting. Lionesses are in each other's faces as well. This greeting ritual enables them to recognize each other. Just as lionesses all look the same to us, so they do to each other. The only way for a lioness to be certain that another lioness is a member of her pride and not an intruder is by smell. As we all know, looks can be deceiving, but smells normally tell the truth.

Each lioness has glands located on her brow, just above her eyes, which secrete the pride's scent. When lionesses regroup, they make intimate social contact by rubbing their cheeks and gently butting heads. This greeting is more than an introduction. An introduction is a first-time encounter that says, "This is who I am. Now who are you?" But a lioness's greeting has the power to strengthen bonds of affection, seal alliances, and expose impostors in the pride's midst.

Lionesses smell and then recognize. Humans recognize first and then smell. Case in point: My husband recently picked me up at the airport. I saw his car coming and began to wave, but it wasn't until he jumped out of the car and collected a hug that I smelled him.

"You smell yummy," I pronounced as I recognized the scent of his cologne.

I can't imagine recognizing him through the reverse process: I see a man jump out of a car and walk toward me. I move in close to smell him, confirm that he smells like my husband, and then I pronounce him mine.

The lionesses' attention to scent recognition serves a number of purposes. The greet-and-groom ritual gives them a natural way to detect when something or someone undesirable has joined the pride. Not only that, when lionesses greet and groom each other, they are showing acceptance and belonging. As God's daughters, we must do the same with the people in our lives.

GREETING AND GROOMING YOUR KIDS

When the lioness greets her cub, she is saying, "You belong with us. You are welcome to be at ease, discover your strengths, and grow up among us. There is provision and safety for you here in the pride." She also uses the greeting to gauge where her cubs have been. Pressing her face close, she detects what the cub has been into, enabling her to ask, "Why am I picking up a trace of hyena on you?"

When my teenage boys went out at night, I required them to give me a good-night kiss when they got home. This kiss served a few purposes. First, I love kissing my boys. Second, I didn't have to stay up to confirm what time they came in. And third, it allowed me to smell them.

The interaction went like this. When the son in question came home, he'd open my bedroom door and say, "I'm home! Good night, Mom."

Because he knew I'd been asleep, he'd close the door quickly. But I would say, "Did you have a good time? Come kiss me."

If he hesitated, then I suspected.

If he came close and I smelled an overpowering scent of mint, I knew he had been doing something less than desirable. When he came near, I reached up and drew him closer in order to detect any secondary smell he might be hiding. After all, a mother knows what her children smell like.

It might have been awkward to get this close to my boys for a late-night check-in if we hadn't already established a daily rhythm of greeting in our home. Our family hugs each other every morning. We embrace throughout the day and kiss each other good night. We have frequent physical contact with each other, whether it comes in the form of wrestling between brothers, jostling during kitchen cleanup, or hugging when we come and go. This process of greeting started when my sons were babies and never stopped. I bet your house is the same—you give each other a kiss good night, a hug hello, a rub on the shoulders, a tousle of the hair, a cuddle on the sofa...

Later on, when my oldest son was out of the house and married, I heard stories of the escapades I'd missed. I asked him, "When did you do that? How did I miss that one?"

He would smile sheepishly and answer, "That happened on a night when you were out of town," or, "That happened when I spent the night at a friend's house."

If I had been home, I would have smelled what he had been up to! Greetings allow moms to ferret out if their kids have had some undesirable contact. This helps us to be in position to respond with love, training, and discipline. If you don't regularly greet one another in your home, I encourage you to begin this practice. Your kids may resist at first, but don't quit. Your hug will not only tell your child that you love him or her; it will also allow you to detect a scent on your child that is not of your house. Mothers, if a child who used to embrace you becomes resistant to your hugs, find out why. Don't allow your child to get comfortable with pulling away from you.

When your children mature and become adults, continue to greet them with hugs and kisses. Your physical affection serves as a reminder that they will always belong to your family. This knowledge gives them security as they transition into adulthood and build families of their own.

GREETING EACH OTHER

When lionesses greet each other, they are saying, "We are related. On you I detect the familiar scent of my sisters. I am here for you, and I know you are here for me."

We are not all that different from our lioness sisters. A warm reception from others says, "Sit with us. You are trusted and welcome." A reception that is formal and guarded communicates, "Your status with us is still under review. Any designation will be reserved until we know you better." In this type of interchange, both greeter and the greeted are ill at ease. If there is no greeting at all, then visitor beware.

Listen to the apostle Paul's words to the Corinthians as he instructs them in the way they should greet one another:

Greet one another with a holy embrace. All the brothers and sisters
here say hello.
The amazing grace of the Master, Jesus Christ, the extravagant
love of God, the intimate friendship of the Holy Spirit, be with all of
you. (2 Corinthians 13:12–14)

When you greet a sister, embrace her as such. If you come in contact with a leader, greet and embrace her in a manner that communicates your appreciation for her. When you greet someone who is hurt, embrace her with your tender concern. Sometimes there don't even have to be words. Over time I have learned a hug is far more healing than a hello.

Paul masterfully wove greetings throughout his letters to the churches in his care. If it was important enough for Paul to put his greeting in writing, then it is certainly important enough for us to put the greeting into practice.

Let's look at his greeting to the church in Corinth:

I'm not writing all this as a neighborhood scold just to make you
feel rotten. *I'm writing as a father to you, my children. I love you and
want you to grow up well, not spoiled.* There are a lot of people around
who can't wait to tell you what you've done wrong, but *there aren't*

many fathers willing to take the time and effort to help you grow up.
(1 Corinthians 4:14–15)

Paul began by telling the Corinthians what his letter was and what it was not. He was not reprimanding them to shame them; rather he defined what his relationship was to them and who they were to him. He was a father, and they were his children. Then Paul explained that although many might watch for the believers in Corinth to fail, as a father he was invested in helping them succeed. His greeting established who he was to the recipients of the letter, who they were to him, what he was saying, why he was saying it, and why they should listen to him. All this was communicated before any message was relayed.

Grooming Each Other

If the ritual of lioness greeting progresses favorably, it quickly morphs into an impromptu grooming session. This mutual grooming forms a solid bond between lionesses and larger cubs, which in turn helps to keep the group closely related and intact.

Lionesses primarily groom each other's head and neck, areas that a lioness would find difficult to reach on her own. With their rough-textured tongues, the lionesses clean off blood and dirt while combing their companion's fur free of ticks and parasites. When something takes blood and nutrients from your body, that creature is slowly but surely stealing your life. While it's good to have blood and dirt removed from our bodies, thank God for aunts and sisters who are willing to pick off ticks and parasites too!

The verb *groom* means to clean, clean up, prepare, brush or brush up, tidy or tidy up, spruce or spruce up, comb, prime, coach, and tutor. According to this definition, I could and should actually groom my teeth, my kitchen, and my children in algebra.

Breaking down the grooming process, it is first defined as "clean" or "clean up." Jesus had a grooming conversation of sorts with Peter. Jesus wanted to bathe Peter's feet. Peter refused. So Jesus let Peter know that if he didn't allow the footbath, then Peter would have no part in what Jesus was doing. Peter overcompensated and took Jesus's offer to the extreme by inviting Jesus to wash him from head to toe. Our amazing Jesus brings it back to the point:

> Jesus said, "If you've had a bath in the morning, you only need your
> feet washed now and you're clean from head to toe.... So now you're
> clean." (John 13:10)

Because we belong to Jesus, we are clean. But even so, in the course of a day, our feet can get dirty, and sometimes, depending on where we've been or what we've done or worn, our feet can even get stinky. As we travel through life, we can step in and through some filthy patches and places—at least I know I can. At the close of day, we need to wash off the dust from the journey of that day.

That's why Jesus goes on to say:

> So if I, the Master and Teacher, washed your feet, you must now
> wash each other's feet. *I've laid down a pattern for you. What I've done,*
> *you do.* I'm only pointing out the obvious. A servant is not ranked
> above his master; an employee doesn't give orders to the employer. If
> you understand what I'm telling you, act like it—and live a blessed
> life. (John 13:14–17)

Jesus washed the feet of his disciples and charged us to do the same with each other. I don't think he literally meant for my husband to give me a mini pedicure each night (though that would be nice, honey). But perhaps the foot washing symbolizes how we can refresh and restore each other, especially when the paths we tread get us dirty.

I've been part of a few awkward foot-washing sessions, particularly during the time when pantyhose were practically a ministry requirement. But back in the days of Jesus, foot washing was a natural part of welcoming people when they entered your home, just as hugging and kissing are now.

I'm not suggesting we reincorporate foot washing. We live in the age of closed shoes and paved streets, and they roamed dusty roads in sandals. I'm suggesting that as we enter the home of a friend or a house of worship, we should take a moment to remove the dust of the day and settle into the relationships to be found there.

Like the lioness, we need each other to clean off the dirt, ticks, and parasites from our lives.

Don't imagine yourself to be quite presentable
    when you haven't had a bath in weeks.

Don't be stuck-up
    and think you're better than everyone else.

Don't be greedy,
    merciless and cruel as wolves,
Tearing into the poor and feasting on them,
    shredding the needy to pieces only to discard them.

A leech has twin daughters
  named "Gimme" and "Gimme more." (Proverbs 30:12–15)

Give me and *give me more* are parasites that diminish our nutrients and rob us of life. Greed and self-indulgence are like vampires. When we are part of a community that grooms one another, we help each other keep our lives clean.

Not long ago I needed to determine whether I had the right to speak into a young man's life. He is a leader with great promise, and I have great respect for him. Because I feel a bit protective of God's call on his life, I wanted to offer him a correction of sorts. But to do this, I first needed to establish what our relationship was, to know if he could hear me. So I asked him, "How do you see me in the church?"

He answered without hesitation, "I see you as a leader."

His response told me that I could speak and that he could correctly hear what I had to say. If he had answered differently, I would have withheld my advice.

This kind of foot washing works both ways. Not only are we to speak into one another's lives; we are to invite others to give their input to us as well. I have a very dear friend who is like a big sister to me. She is a pastor extraordinaire and a seasoned gatherer of God's daughters. We have been close friends long enough for her to know both my strengths and weaknesses.

Recently I felt I needed to intentionally invite her to be part of the grooming process in my life. Over a cup of coffee, I told her, "I need you to speak into my life. If you see or hear me say or do something stupid or out of order, please tell me. In no way do I feel that I have arrived spiritually or that I am above correction, but I need someone who is qualified to speak direction and wisdom into my life."

She graciously agreed to groom any unsightly areas of my life. For this to actually happen, I have to be in relationship with her. I intentionally maintain contact with her and sit under her instruction by reading her books and listening to her podcasts. (There is no reason she should have to repeat for me what she has already clearly outlined.) She has no desire to control me, only to make sure I don't have dirt on my face! When we are all part of a social grooming dynamic, we understand that if we are muddy, it reflects on other sisters as well.

If you enter a house of worship and there is no greeting or establishment of relationship for you, I encourage you to find a church where there is interaction and connection. Friendships and churches without connection and interaction will not groom you for God's purposes. When we need grooming, it becomes evident. I invited my pastor friend to speak into my life because I realized that I needed this type of grooming. I was feeling isolated and misunderstood. These are not attractive accessories, and I knew I needed the insightful help of another to comb and remove them from my life.

This grooming process can be a major point of connection for us. It seems our large feline friends know innately what we humans often learn at great expense: it can be dangerous to groom yourself.

HOLINESS, NOT HYGIENE

You will remember that Peter protested the foot wash and then volunteered for the body cleanse, until Jesus let him know he didn't need to be so fastidious. Jesus told him:

My concern, you understand, is holiness, not hygiene. (John 13:10)

Jesus's concern should be our own—holiness, not hygiene. At the end of the day, this is what we are responsible for. When self is our focus, greed and indulgence run rampant. Some Christians are consumed with maintaining an appearance of holiness while they accuse others of being unclean. Jesus was talking about this very issue when he said:

> For you are so careful to clean the outside of the cup and the dish, but inside you are filthy—full of greed and self-indulgence! (Matthew 23:25, NLT)

We should not miss the bigger picture here: holiness is not a function of hygiene as much as it is of the heart. The course of our daily life may dirty our hands and feet, but it cannot make dirty what God alone makes clean. He alone is the Lord God who makes us holy!

Confusion happens when our focus is on avoiding bad rather than on doing good. It is then that our vacant lives run the risk of being invaded by unwanted intruders and predators. Jesus went about doing good, not avoiding bad. The opposite of sin is virtue.

Evil is overcome with good. Evil is not displaced by rules or by hiding from it. Yes, we should have boundaries and use wisdom. Yes, we should not participate in or with evil. But are we scrubbing what doesn't need to be removed? Let's not try to wash ourselves and others clean of the wrong things.

Here was Jesus's advice for cleansing the body of greed and self-indulgence.

> So *clean the inside* by giving gifts to the poor, and you will be clean all over. (Luke 11:41, NLT)

God's concern is that we are clean on the inside. He has been encouraging me to exhort his body, the church, that it is time to get some dirt under our nails and on our clothes as we reach outside our overly clean buildings and help others.

This was a lesson that Simon the Pharisee needed to learn.

THE ULTIMATE GROOMING ACT

Jesus was invited to dine at Simon the Pharisee's house. It was a gathering of the "clean" until the town harlot burst in. She heard that Jesus would be there, and she showed up. If that wasn't bad enough, she took out a vial of expensive perfume, knelt down before Jesus, and in tears poured the perfume all over his feet! Poor Simon. All he wanted was a nice dinner party for Jesus and his friends, and this happened. When Simon saw this, he said to himself, "If this man was the prophet I thought he was, he would have known what kind of woman this is who is falling all over him" (Luke 7:39).

Jesus then asked Simon a question. He wanted to know who would be more grateful over a debt cancellation: the person who owed a little or the one who owed a lot. Simon correctly answered that the one who had been forgiven more would be more grateful.

Suddenly Jesus addressed the elephant (or harlot) in the room:

Then turning to the woman, but speaking to Simon, he said, "Do you see this woman? I came to your home; you provided no water for my feet, but she rained tears on my feet and dried them with her hair. You gave me no greeting, but from the time I arrived she hasn't quit kissing my feet. You provided nothing for freshening up, but she has soothed my feet with perfume. *Impressive, isn't it?* She was forgiven many, many sins, and so she is very, very grateful. If the forgiveness is minimal, the gratitude is minimal." (Luke 7:43–47)

These verses are a record of what Jesus said *about this woman* in the presence of the religious experts, but even more significant are the words he said *to her.*

Then he spoke to her: *"I forgive your sins."*

That set the dinner guests talking behind his back: "Who does he think he is, forgiving sins!"

He ignored them and said to the woman, "Your faith has saved you. Go in peace." (Luke 7:48–50)

It is notable that Jesus gave this release to the one person who had not been invited to the party. Why? Because unlike Simon, she greeted him and washed his feet. Simon had positioned himself too high to humble himself before Jesus—but not this woman.

Was forgiveness of sin available to Simon? Of course. It was available to all in attendance. Jesus declared as much in the parable he shared, but in that moment Simon didn't realize or recognize his need for the heart grooming that Jesus could provide.

When we imagine that we are above the need for heart grooming, we start judging others. In judgment we deny others what we ourselves need. This is what happened to Simon. He needed his feet washed. He needed the greeting of peace. He needed the healing of an anointing balm. But since he thought he was above needing these things, he did not offer any of these rituals of greeting and grooming to his guests.

A PLACE OF HONOR

As I write this, I can't help but wonder if Jesus has turned his face to the women as he poses a question to the legalistic leaders of our day, asking something like this: "You think the sin of the woman is too great for her to merit acknowledgment, so you ignore her. You imagine she is in some way less than in my charge to present the gospel, but I have highlighted the example of this woman—and thus exonerated women. You imagine Eve's sin to be greater than Adam's, and therefore you deny her daughters access to my table, but don't forget that those who are forgiven much are all the more grateful. A place of honor will be found for these daughters, even if it is by way of washing and anointing my feet."

Lovely lionesses, it is time we again give our glorious Lord something to brag about. To see this happen, I am willing to wash some feet and have mine washed. Let's each be willing to do anything or go anywhere if it means Jesus will have reason to marvel when he looks our way. Simon thought this loose woman was falling all over Jesus, but Jesus called her awkward attempts lovely. Don't worry if your attempts are awkward at first. Just commit to begin. I want us all to make this kind of impression on Jesus so that he would say of us, "I am impressed they have shown me so much love."

Let's do something wonderfully significant for our Lord. As we lavish kindness, grooming, and welcome on others, we pour out our adoration on him. Let's anoint one another for his return and our resurrection. Let's wash each other's feet, even if it is with our tears. Let them fall unhindered until there is enough moisture to wash the dust and filth off the feet of the church. Let's weep over our own sins and cry over the injustice levied on our sisters and children the world over. If the mercy that has been lavished on you is not enough to reduce you to tears, then allow the cruelty of the plight of captive daughters to move you. Your tears wash the feet of others and magnify our Lord.

The lioness greeting and grooming is symbolic of how we show acceptance and belonging to one another. How we greet indicates how we see one another (as leaders, peers, or disciples). How others see you determines how you will be groomed. The lioness example shows us that we add value when we groom others. In this recognition, we exhibit honor, humility, and respect. Our greeting should say, "I know you. I value you. I'm here for you. Now about the mud from that rough place, let me help you wash that off."

I just returned from two days with my regular gathering of lionesses. When we meet, we embrace. We are comfortable and comforted by the presence of one another. The six of us occupied two hotel rooms. We fell asleep and woke together. Throughout the day we shared lattes and meals. We gathered in pajamas and greeted and groomed one another late into the night. We have learned to be open and to freely share who we are with one another. Among this sweet core of friends are heartbroken mothers, an unsettled sojourner, a weary warrior, and an excited visionary.

We spent our first night greeting each other. (I love you. I've missed you.) And we woke the next day to begin the process of grooming. (How are you?) We know each other's strengths and weaknesses. We understand that sometimes these are one and the same. We ask each other hard questions. Together we laugh, cry, pray, and confess fears, sins, and weaknesses. We close by praying for one another and our children and futures. I come away exhausted but with ticks removed, dust brushed off, and my feet washed.

I have learned to embrace the grooming process because I know these sister lionesses love me and are there for me. I know who they are in my life, and they know who I am in theirs. Sometimes we disagree, but that doesn't mean we disband.

Who are the women in your life that need to be greeted? Who in your world would benefit from some tender grooming? Is there someone you could invite to be a part of your grooming process?

Lionesses Are Strategic

Energy and insights of justice to those who
guide and decide, strength and prowess to
those who guard and protect.

ISAIAH 28:6

Lionesses are not the strongest savanna creatures, but what they lack in strength, they make up for in strategy and heart. Our lioness sisters work together as a strategic team of related females. There are pride sisters, aunts, mothers, daughters, and cousins. They are all loosely related and therefore well acquainted with one another's strengths and weaknesses. When it comes to hunting for food, searching for a lost cub, or training and protecting the young, every lioness in the pride has her role and contributions.

Let's begin with the dynamic of the hunt. Three significant factors come into play when lionesses hunt: timing, camouflage, and proximity. For the lioness, timing is not just crucial—it's everything. She has learned a skill we'd do well to adopt: allow timing to work in your favor. The lioness works with the elements of timing and lighting to know when to hunt. She hunts when her environment is the most favorable—at dusk and predawn. No one can rush a sunset or delay the sun's rise, so lionesses are patient and intentional. Reduced light optimizes her camouflage, which grants her proximity. With nightfall the vision of most animals on the African plain decreases, while the lioness's sight remains intact (more on that later).

With the lighting in her favor, she then works timing and placement into the equation as well.

For the most part, lionesses hide in the open. They appear somewhat casual in the light of day as they position themselves downwind on the fringe of their prey. Once a lioness locates her prime position, she drops.

The lioness's effect on the herd is far from casual. Her presence ripples through the plain, and those closest panic and scatter. The frightened animals turn to see if the lioness has given chase. But the lioness hasn't moved. It's not time. She is still and almost imperceptible in the golden grass. She may nap as she waits, but her sleep isn't deep. She's just gathering strength as she waits for the right moment to make a move.

The skittish herd calms, and the lioness is forgotten. Heads drop as they return to grazing. With practiced patience the lioness has become part of the landscape, and her prey relaxes and becomes dangerously comfortable with her presence. She's achieved the atmosphere of nonchalance she had hoped for. Now the lioness becomes intentional.

As dusk approaches, the lioness creeps closer, slow and low to the ground. Her huge paws are virtually soundless. Head low, she takes measured pauses to gauge the distance to her prey. Surprise and proximity are crucial if her pounce is to be successful. She is no match for the impala's speed.

Suddenly the lioness bursts from the brush. The terrified impala leaps away; its hindquarters barely miss being shredded by the lioness's sharp claws. The chase is on. Caught up in the terror of the moment, the impala does not know it is headed for an ambush. Another lioness heads him off. He turns to avoid her and runs into the path of yet another lioness. The kill is quick and almost humane.

Did our first lioness miss? Maybe, maybe not, but one thing is certain—she was part of a carefully executed strategic plan. Lionesses are the only large cats who hunt as one. Tigers, leopards, panthers, and cheetahs hunt solo, but lionesses hunt together. They are highly skilled huntresses. Each lioness takes her position and perfects her hunting skills in the company of her pride's sisters. Male lions have been known to rush into a herd in an attempt to take down whatever they can. A lion is after all a formidable killer. But lionesses do not rush…they dance. Their coordinated hunt is breathtaking. This is the reason the lioness is considered *the height of hunting prowess.*

PROWESS

I love this word *prowess*. I love the way it feels when I say it. Go ahead, try it…prrrrrowwwwessss.

For a while now, I've been intentionally introducing the word *prowess* into conversations. It never fails to raise eyebrows. *Prowess* hasn't been over-used and rung dry of its original meaning like other words. Like the lioness, *prowess* carries a measure of wonder and within its letters an aura of mystery.

The young women who travel with me have been known to use this word in a variety of pairings to see how it fits. They speak of travel *prowess,* baggage *prowess,* packing *prowess,* and prayer and preaching *prowess.* We want *prowess* to be the new cool word.

On a more serious note, *prowess* has meanings I want women to explore and express. In addition to coupling the term *hunting* with *prowess* (as in the lioness is the height of hunting prowess), I'd like to see it paired with words like *fierce, strategic, innovative, parenting, style,* and *communication.*

The options are potentially endless. But the lioness doesn't *talk* prowess—she *is* prowess.

If prowess had a form, it would definitely be feline. Even though I am a dog person, I can't imagine assigning the term *prowess* to my Yorkie. If prowess had a color, I'd imagine it golden. A texture? Rippling fur. Prowess would walk with purpose and, when necessary, sleek stealth. Prowess cannot be forced or faked, but it can and should be developed. If you have it, you own it. Prowess is what makes the lioness powerful. She's not frightened by her strength. On the contrary, it comforts her.

According to my laptop's Encarta thesaurus, *prowess* encompasses the terms *ability, skill, expertise, competence, dexterity, aptitude,* and *proficiency.* In addition I love this double-edged definition: "1. exceptional ability, skill, or strength; 2. exceptional valor or bravery."[1]

Like the lioness, you too have prowess. There is exceptional ability, strength, or valor waiting to be realized in your life. It may be in hiding, waiting to be encouraged to develop, but never doubt that it is there. God hides talents and abilities deep within each of us. Our quest is to unearth and hone them. Prowess might say, *I don't know or do everything, but what I know, I choose to do well.* Areas of prowess are often awakened through the medium of play, such as games, sports, or make-believe. Is there something within you that wants to come out and play? Your area of prowess may be what's excited when you see lionesses unafraid and in action. Whether they are hunting, protecting, or training, they do what they know well.

And why are lionesses considered the height of hunting prowess? They hunt *together,* without competition and without breaking rank. No woman's portion or contribution is more significant than another's. We need you to *be you*! Duplicating the talents of another serves no one well, least of all you. Individuality is not born through comparison, copying, or competition. Each lioness hones her own skill set. We would do well to follow her example.

> So since we find ourselves fashioned into all these excellently formed and marvelously functioning parts in Christ's body, *let's just go ahead and be what we were made to be*, without enviously or pridefully comparing ourselves with each other, or trying to be something we aren't. (Romans 12:5–6)

Often I am part of conferences composed of highly gifted speakers. It can be intimidating to follow one of their presentations. Through trial and error I have learned the best course is just to be the best version of me. Remember, no one invites you into their world in order for you to pretend to be someone else. They want you.

When I read "excellently formed and marvelously functioning" in the scripture above, I am reminded of our term *prowess* and the fact that your very creation expresses both fear and wonder. God did not breathe a spirit of fear into you but a spirit of love, power, and clarity of mind (see 2 Timothy 1:7, NKJV). You were created fearfully, not afraid and fearful. You, lovely one, were positioned on earth in a season of worldwide terror to express the wonder of our God. You are called to be a marvelously functioning part, which, in my opinion, is another expression of prowess.

God is inviting one and all to take their positions, like the lioness, everyone in their place, everyone in their strength.

The lioness's hunting supremacy is celebrated in many African cultures. Notable warriors or hunters earn the designation of "son of the lioness." You see, it is the lioness who trains the cubs, both male and female, to hunt. The Scriptures even highlight this dynamic:

> What a lioness was your mother
> > among lions!
> She crouched in a pride of young lions.
> > Her cubs grew large.
> She reared one of her cubs to maturity,
> > a robust young lion.
> He learned to hunt. (Ezekiel 19:2–3)

But the lionesses' care is not limited to their young; many animals do this. Lionesses have been known to care for the older or injured lionesses in the pride as well. They're the glue that keeps the pride functioning as a healthy unit.

The male lion is a prominent figure who is not afraid to make his presence known. In contrast, the lioness's strength is in her ability to almost disappear. It does not serve her purpose to declare her presence during a hunt, and when it comes to providing for her young, camouflage is a decided advantage. If her young are threatened, however, that's another story.

> Can you teach the lioness to stalk her prey
> > and satisfy the appetite of her cubs
> As they crouch in their den? (Job 38:39)

This scripture is a listen-in on God and Job conversing. This interchange reveals that God is the one who teaches the lioness to hunt, stalk, and provide for her waiting cubs. I wonder how this is accomplished. Does our magnificent God place clues and cues in the lioness's environment that continually hone her skills? Do God-breathed elements of creation teach the lioness to hunt and nurture, just as creation's wonder awakens our desire to seek God and love one another?

A Wild Chase

I want to expand your concept of the hunt. A hunt is not limited to *Kill, then eat. Hunt* also describes a chase, a search, or even a rescue. The verb form means to chase, pursue, stalk, hound, follow, or lie in wait for. I find it interesting that these verbs are used to describe our pursuit of God.

> GOD! God! I am running to you for dear life;
>   the chase is wild. (Psalm 7:1)

This hunt is exciting. I love the concept of a "wild God chase." This description is a far cry from half-asleep morning quiet time. These words imply urgency, speed, and focused pursuit. This scripture could be approached from another angle as well. It could be an account of escaping *from* something wild and dangerous—or a chase through the wild *to* God. Both work. Both are exciting, though I prefer the idea of a wild, dangerous God chase. I also like the idea that he might wildly pursue me. Sometimes as I look at the mountain range framed by my front window, I whisper, "God, who are you? I want to know myself in light of your rugged might!"

Surely no one imagines they can hunt God. It would be ludicrous even to consider knocking him off balance. We do catch a glimpse though. Hidden in him is whatever I might seek. Lovely one, I have never sensed such an urgent call to the hunt. It's time for a wild pursuit of God.

Just as the lioness waits in patience, a timed wait is part of our pursuit of God. The psalmist wrote:

Listen to my voice in the morning, LORD.
    Each morning I bring my requests to you and wait expectantly.
        (Psalm 5:3, NLT)

Hunt also means "look, search, or seek after." These echo all we've relayed. Lastly, *hunt* denotes a search, quest, pursuit, or expedition.

As daughters of the Most High God, we hunt for answers, wisdom, and strength. We chase God that he might catch us; once captured, we will reflect his light and life to others.

Your beauty and love chase after me
    every day of my life.
I'm back home in the house of GOD
    for the rest of my life. (Psalm 23:6)

Wisdom and counsel can be found in the company of women who've not only chased after God but who have been chased by God. Each of these wildly awakened women has a portion of God's love and compassion to express to others. The earth is waiting to see what happens when God's beauty and love have not only captured but mobilized a company of women. You, lovely one, are part of an expedition for truth and a revelation of solutions. Our quest for divine God-connections ultimately comes through a revelation of our lion, Jesus. There are questions women alone know how to ask. There are answers God has entrusted us to reveal. To see this accomplished, we gather.

Before our lioness sisters hunt, they gather. They rest together, hunger together, stretch and rise up together. Together they take their hunting positions, and when it's over, they feast together. Then the cycle repeats itself. Positions may change, but ultimately lionesses are together!

Margaret Mead was a brilliant cultural anthropologist who made this observation after many years immersed in diverse cultures: "Sister is probably the most competitive relationship within the family, but once the sisters are grown, it becomes the strongest relationship."[2]

As I read these words, I thought, *This is what is happening! We are growing up!*

As I wrote and researched my book *Nurture,* I noticed the lack of biblical examples of sisters doing life together strategically. In fact, I was disheartened, wondering where I could find a model for women who were friends and confidantes. I was desperate to know. You see, we will not rise like lionesses unless the Spirit of God guides us through the process.

While I searched the Scriptures for an example, I sensed God's Spirit whisper, *The chapter of the daughters is being written right now. Tell my daughters to write their lives well!*[3]

I don't want to run the risk of you not knowing how crucial and integral your contribution is. Do you understand what this means? We are individually and cooperatively writing the story of God's daughters, a related company of sisters who gather to write their lives well and who make each word, action, and choice count. With this gathering I see his lionesses rising in fierce strength, grace, and skill.

Pursuing Justice

Not only do we rise together in the pursuit of God and his answers; it's time we rise in our pursuit of justice. Justice does not require a legal degree. Justice should be a lifestyle. Our nation was founded as a haven from the ravages of injustice. Our legal system established our courts as sanctuaries for truth. Recent rulings would give us cause to wonder if they are dramatic playgrounds for cunning lawyers.

> Energy and insights of justice to those who guide and decide,
>> strength and prowess to those who guard and protect. (Isaiah 28:6)

This scripture lends remarkable insight. Justice is more than executing a list of rules. It requires thought and energy. We need wisdom's insight so both judge and jury settle on verdicts that will ultimately guide a nation and the actions of its citizens from injustice to justice. The maintenance of true justice calls for strong and excellent protectors.

There was a time when *justice* was used to describe our nation. When I was growing up, one of our superhero's slogans was "Truth, justice, and the American way."

> Judgment will again be founded on justice,
>> and those with virtuous hearts will pursue it. (Psalm 94:15, NLT)

We need a revival of justice. I fear our judicial system has lost its sense of righteous judgment. Virtuous hearts pursue justice. When your heart is right, injustice becomes abhorrent to you. This is not limited to the judicial system; it should span every walk of life. While we wait for the government, the church, or someone else to make the wrong in our world right, women and children are dying. At the bare minimum I think we can all agree that justice involves rescuing children from harm.

Using their prowess, lionesses work together to protect the pride's cubs. If the cubs are threatened, the lioness becomes a strategic warrior. I watched a documentary where a cobra had managed to position itself within a pride of lions. The lionesses remained calm even though a deadly cobra was in their midst. Their response was a calm, orderly, and immediate evacuation of the cubs to a safe alternate site. Each grabbed the nearest cub by the scruff of the neck and quickly put distance between their young and the lethal snake. One lioness stayed with the cubs while her sisters returned to join those who'd stayed behind to track the snake's movements.

I was impressed that these lionesses were wise enough to know not to engage a cobra with their young nearby. The cubs would not only have been at risk; they would have been in the way. With the cubs safe, it was time to confront the cobra. The lionesses' instinctual approach was highly tactical and strategic.

Lionesses are fiercely protective of *all* their pride's young. A lioness will not endanger another lioness's cub any more than she'd endanger her own. Lionesses don't merely hunt together; they mother together. Likewise, we should be committed to putting distance between all the earth's children and whatever endangers or threatens their lives. It is not enough to be concerned with our own. This means we wage battles at home and abroad. Let's arise for our neighbors, both near and far.

In lionesses this drive to protect is so strong that they have the cubs' protection in mind even before conception. Through some God-breathed provision of nature, lionesses have the ability to synchronize their estrous or reproductive cycle. This allows them to conceive and give birth together.

So, in essence, the pride itself becomes pregnant. Lionesses realize that cubs of similar age have a greater chance of survival due to equal access to food and training. All these golden babies tumbling around means there is no lack of nursing mothers. Because the pride consists of related females, the lionesses will nurse and train one another's young. There is great advantage in growing up alongside pride brothers and sisters of similar experience and size. It means there are similar rhythms in the patterns of sparring, feeding, resting, and playing that ultimately translate to complementary skill levels, which helps the survival of not only the cubs but also their future pride.

Lionesses train their young by modeling what is correct. In the wild there is little margin for error. If skills sets are not transferred, the survival of the cubs is threatened and the legacy of the pride compromised.

Lionesses learn how to hunt through play. While still cubs, they learn the elements. The mama lionesses lay around as the young ones pounce and play. The mothers join in as well. Lionesses not only wrestle with the cubs; they play well with each other. They allow the cubs to feel powerful as they tumble, tackle, and bounce around. If they go too far, a mama lioness is always nearby to provide a growl or cuff to the one that gets out of hand.

All this frolicking playtime serves a purpose as it inevitably highlights the strengths of each pride member. God loves it when we laugh and engage in recreation. We could say we involve ourselves in a "re-create" when we play.

Because you've always stood up for me,
    I'm free to run and play. (Psalm 63:7)

When I first learned that lionesses conceive and give birth together in order to share in the feeding and training of their young, I heard the Spirit of God whisper, *Lisa, every child deserves an equal chance of survival. Every child needs to be protected, nurtured, trained, and provided for.* The welfare of the earth's children is our post. We need to be strategic in our pursuit of justice for them.

A FIERCE RESPONSE

How much more should the human mother rescue children who are not her own?

> Can a mother forget her nursing child?
> Can she feel no love for the child she has borne?
> *But even* if that were possible,
> I would not forget you! (Isaiah 49:15, NLT)

It is so unimaginable that a mother could forget her child that the living God said, "even if that were possible." This verse underscores how unnatural it is for women to fail to nurture or to knowingly hurt a child. Sadly, we live in a day when the unthinkable has become reality. With increasing frequency the news carries stories of mothers who compromise the safety and welfare of their children in exchange for drugs, alcohol, or money.

Recently the media highlighted the plight of two young girls who had been kidnapped by different couples. One brave girl was held captive for eighteen years, and during this harrowing time, she birthed and nurtured two daughters. The other young girl was kidnapped from her family home and held for nine months. Both of these young women were raped and brutalized by vicious predators. In both cases the childless wife was charged as an accomplice to her husband's crimes.

When my son Alec realized women were involved, he was shocked. "Why didn't the wives rescue the young girls?" he asked, unable to fathom a world where women did not rescue children.

All I could answer was that neither of these women was healthy. They had choices, and they chose to remain silent. For some reason a mother's heart had not awakened in either of them.

We tend to think women are oppressed by men, but this is not always the case. These women knew what was going on and did nothing. In fact, they enabled the abuse of these girls.

It is interesting to note that both male abusers twisted scriptures and used unhealthy views of submission to manipulate their wives and the girls. Wanting to please their husbands, the wives' complicity shocked a nation.

In contrast, a lioness will put herself between her cubs and harm's way. I have read accounts in which lionesses even worked together against the lions of their pride if their actions threatened the pride's young.

There has never been a more critical time for us to be healthy women who rightly divide and live the Word of God. We must establish a wise and thoughtful view of issues such as gender, submission, and unconditional marital obedience. God never meant any of these principles to put others at risk. They were meant for health and good.

It is our responsibility to protect the young and vulnerable. Like the lioness, we should always seek to move children out of harm's way. Lionesses understand by God-given instinct what some women have forgotten: mothers rescue even if the child is not their own.

Apparently just giving birth doesn't make you a mother. A few months ago our nation was aghast at the story of a beautiful, smiling five-year-old girl whose mother sold her into sexual servitude. They found the young girl's body in a wooded area off a rural road in North Carolina. I shudder to think what else might be in the news by the time this book is in print.

I thank God that for most of us, this type of maternal disconnect is still unthinkable. The Scriptures predict there will be a brutish time when people who have lost their way will forget what it is to be human (see Romans 1:26). To be human is to be godlike and to have within us a conscience and measure of his heart. God is outraged by this devaluing of life and sexualizing of children who are made in his image. Knowing this is his response, we should likewise respond with a fierce and loving reaction. Some of us need to open our homes by way of adoption and take the at-risk or unwanted children in. We need to be generous and not depend on the government to make right what we see as wrong. Let's truly love our neighbors.

If we remain silent in the face of oppression and injustice, we run the risk that it will one day overtake us. I long to see the church rise up to put right the injustices of human trafficking and the sex-slave trade. They are never far from my mind and are often present in my speech. Recently I told a young woman seated next to me on a flight about my passion to see women the world over mobilized into some form of action that confronted these issues. She turned toward me and demanded, "By what authority do you speak to this matter?"

The intensity of her question caught me completely off guard. Stunned, I paused, then countered, "By what authority would I dare to remain *silent*?"

Dropping her voice, she tried to explain that she wanted to know if I had any educational or professional qualifications. I held her gaze and explained that, the last time I checked, there was no law against raising your voice against injustice, and from what I've seen, there is no single "professional" answer. The enormity of these crimes will require the response of many.

It is a gross injustice to strip children of their innocence and enslave them to the lust and debauchery of an adult. How can *any of us* remain silent when the voices of so many children have been silenced?

How can we not cry out over this issue? How many times must we hear "All that is necessary for the triumph of evil is for good men to do nothing" before we will not only believe it but act on it? When I am overseas and walking through places of dire poverty, I look into the eyes of the mothers and wonder what they must be thinking. Are they asking, *Is my child less valuable than yours?*

God forbid that we should allow them to believe this. When I was in Southeast Asia, twice a mother offered me her child. One mother went as far as to put her child in my arms. As I held him, she looked at me and gestured as she spoke words I couldn't understand. After I had complimented the beauty of another mother's baby, she asked through the interpreter if I wanted her daughter. Do you see their desperation? They tried to give their children to me, a total stranger who didn't even speak their language. Perhaps they hoped for money, but I believe more than this they wanted hope for their children. To sell a child is unthinkable in our culture, but what would you do if you had nothing left to give your child?

Will we raise our children so they are mindful that they share the world and its resources with these women's children? I believe God wants you and me to do just that by bringing it home.

RESCUING THE CHILDREN

Yes, there is overwhelming heartbreak in countries where poverty strips the human soul, but there are battles on local levels that require our attention as well. As I wrote this book, an interesting incident occurred. I caught a glimpse of what strategic prowess might look like if applied to a local educational system. I say a glimpse because my involvement was merely a visit, and I respectfully realize there are many who are vigilant and actively involved in the educational systems and processes. I thank God for teachers and educational administrators who work tirelessly to provide quality education on tight budgets. This is why there are times they need our help.

One weeknight my youngest son, Arden, had some reading homework to tackle. Because he was super tired from basketball tryouts, he asked if I would mind reading to him. He was afraid he'd fall asleep if he attempted it on his own. The rest of the family was in the great room, noisily engaged with a football game, so we escaped to my bedroom.

As we read, I grew increasingly alarmed by the book's content. There was an assortment of thoughts of teen suicide, vandalism, spouse and child abuse, violence, underage drinking, alcoholism, parental abandonment, and shoplifting. Just when I thought it couldn't get any worse, we came to a highly objectionable sexual passage.

My son turned and said, "Mom, I don't want to read this book anymore." He then told me there were other passages that were equally offensive. The problem was, this book was required reading for the freshman boys in his literature class. I determined I would call the school in the morning and request that Arden be assigned another book to read. The next morning when I spoke with the teacher, she agreed that Arden could read an alternative book for this assignment. I hung up, thinking all was well, but later that day some things happened that convinced me I needed to do more. According to school policy, due to its objectionable material, this book required parental permission. I realized the other parents had no idea what was in this book. After all, the only reason I was aware was because I had read it to my son. Under normal conditions I wouldn't have known either.

Was it right that only my son was protected from its content? How would this book frame perspectives on pornography, sex, parents, alcohol, stealing, violence, and suicide for the other boys in the class? Knowing what I did, could I remain silent? Wasn't it my responsibility to protect these other children and parents as well?

I wrote a blog to raise awareness about the content and gathered support to alert the school that I was not alone in my concern. In less than twenty-four hours, more than five hundred people (many of them educators) responded, saying that they too had found the book inappropriate. Some were homeschooling mothers who said this type of thing was the very reason they'd pulled their children out of public school.

I wasn't questioning the author's right to pen his story. My concern was that this book was required reading for fourteen-year-olds. This book advocated pornography. Sex trafficking has its beginning in pornography. Unhealthy images can literally skew a young man's perception of women in unimaginable ways. The book in question made it appear that pornography coupled with masturbation was normal behavior for fourteen-year-old boys. Pornography has the power to create a mind-set that subjugates and ensnares its victims (male and female). This violation can taint future sexual interaction with misogyny, emotional and sexual detachment, and sexual addiction—all of which pave the way to sex trafficking.

I knew our local educational system hoped to inspire virtue in their young men and women. They had effective policies in place to uphold this goal, but somehow this book had slipped through. I made an appointment with the principal of the school to alert him that some policies had been broken. I shared my concern that as someone who'd seen firsthand the fallout of sex trafficking, I was alarmed by the introduction of women as sex objects.

Within the week the book was pulled. They were glad an error in the selection process had been discovered and made some changes so future book selections would not hit these snags.

Public schools are staffed with people committed to educating children. Just like any of us, they can make mistakes and have lapses in judgment. Rather than attack them, isn't it better to come alongside as an ally in the education process and to encourage the best for *all* children rather than just protect our own?

After I voiced my concern, the school realized this book was slated for all the freshmen classes, and my son's class just happened to be the first to read it. Because an alarm was raised and the school was supportive, a lot of children were spared the violation of reading offensive and questionable material.

Throughout this process I did not pull the Christian card. I did not rant and rave at the school's teachers or administration. I appealed to them according to their own set of policies. In addition to pointing out a problem, I suggested a reasonable solution. I let them know I was committed to the process of seeing this through. Any one of you could do the same.

It's Time to Hunt

God is inviting you and me to be part of a hunt. As we seek and pursue him, we will find the wisdom and answers we need. In a world torn apart by divorce and emotional detachment, we need heaven-breathed friendships and strategic relationships in order to train and protect each other's children. To realize the rescue of the lost and at-risk children of our world, heaven-breathed strategies and answers will need to be implemented. No one is an island. We are in this together. Because of this dynamic, what you do has the power to affect me, and what I do has the power to affect you. With coordinated efforts we have a chance to turn the tide in our homes, churches, and communities. We live in a time when there is great opportunity for social networking. It is up to us to decide if we will use these connections for good.

When I began researching the lioness, I did not realize lions are the only members of the cat family that live in community. Where one lioness is weak, another is strong. Where one might falter, another succeeds, and all this strength happens in the shelter of the mighty lion.

This is not the case for solitary cats. The mighty panther, leopard, or cheetah has no such support system. Each time these mothers leave their litter behind to hunt and search for food, they run the risk of returning to a den that has been ravaged. In one documentary I heard the pitiful cries of a mother cheetah that had returned to her den only to discover her young were gone. Her voice was pitiful as she called to them all night in the hope one had somehow escaped the carnage.

You and I were never made for isolation. I can't even begin to express what an amazing source of comfort it has been to have people outside my family watch over my children as though they were their own. We have been blessed with people who lift my family before God's throne and guard us in prayer. Even those I've never met have prayed on our behalf, and only later have we heard about it. Many have given generously to see the gospel furthered and captives they will never meet rescued. May heaven abundantly reward each of you who watch over the families of others.

TAKE HIS AIR

When the lioness does kill, more often than not, she does not tear or rend her prey. She suffocates it by blocking off its air passages. Likewise, I believe it's time we too block the enemy's air supply. One way we can do this is to stop lending him our breath. Too frequently we give him too much to work with. We should cut off his force by not speaking against one another. Instead, let's skillfully use our words to build, admonish, correct, and encourage.

In this hunt I *need* other women who understand my strengths and undergird my weaknesses—and so do you. To accomplish this, I have chosen to intentionally surround myself with people who are strong where I am weak. It is my earnest prayer that I may lend these friends my strength in their areas of weakness. Healthy, balanced relationships are those where each member has a contribution.

May none of us be content with the safety of our children alone but instead grow in the understanding and awareness that all the children of this earth are our charge. May we be careful to move all children out of harm's way. May none of us imagine that local influence does not have the potential for far-reaching impact. Let none of us believe that our role is inconsequential. And let none of us imagine we can conquer the world single-handedly.

> Stand united, singular in vision, contending for people's trust in the
> Message, the good news, not flinching or dodging in the slightest
> before the opposition. Your courage and unity will show them what
> they're up against: defeat for them, victory for you—and both
> because of God. (Philippians 1:27–28)

Together we can be strategic.

Lionesses Live in the Light and Hunt in the Dark

> The wicked are edgy with guilt, ready to run off
> even when no one's after them;
> Honest people are relaxed and confident,
> bold as lions.
>
> PROVERBS 28:1

Not only do lionesses innately know what they are capable of and how to do what they do well (prowess!), but their lives are relatively uncomplicated. They rest when tired and hunt and eat when they are hungry. Outside of that, they mainly play!

You may have seen lionesses lounging around as though half asleep. Sometimes they even flip on their backs as they rest in the golden sunlight—like solar panels storing up energy for later. Even the bouncing cubs barely elicit a response from resting lionesses. Occasionally a cub might cross a barrier and receive a halfhearted swat from the nearest mama. But no one seems stressed as they nap an average of twenty hours a day.

After rest time lionesses may be seen stretching and joining in group play as they transition into their secondary posture—high alert. However, even in a state of high alert, they are focused but never stressed.

This focused yet relaxed posture is another crucial element of the lioness's prowess we daughters need to adopt. The following scripture lends us some insight.

> The wicked are edgy with guilt, ready to run off
> even when no one's after them;
> Honest people are relaxed and confident,
> bold as lions. (Proverbs 28:1)

There it is—relaxed, confident, and bold. People don't normally pair relaxed and confident with bold, but God does. I can see it in the lioness. Her posture constantly communicates, "I am what I am. I am powerful and highly skilled, playful and deadly, relaxed, focused, and nurturing."

Like any woman, the lioness is a collection of contradictions. Even though this verse refers to lions, its reference is gender inclusive. All lions—male and female—have this attitude. Perhaps it should become ours as well.

When our lioness isn't hunting, she has no reason to move about in the shadows. She lives in the light. She gathers with her sisters and does life right out in the open, light-filled expanses of the African plain. There, in a realm without shade, they rest, play, groom, feed, train, and even mate in the open. But *why* would a lioness feel any shame or the need to hide?

In their world there is no enemy bold or powerful enough to openly challenge them in combat. They back down before no one (other than giving way to elephants when they come barreling through). And when the lioness is not positioned to hunt, she has little or no need for camouflage. Lions are the undisputed kings and queens of their domain and at the top of their community food chain.

If the day is especially hot, the lioness may choose to rest in the shade, but she does not take cover in order to hide. Unlike the leopard and cheetah, who live and hunt alone, there is no need for the lioness to scale trees or crouch in underbrush, even though she is capable of doing both. No, our lioness rests unafraid in the full light of day surrounded by sisters, aunts, mother, and cousins, along with her young and her lion.

Even as I write this, I want it. I want to rest unafraid in the sun among sisters, daughters, cousins, and mothers as we all smile at the young, content with the full understanding that there is nothing in our present environment capable of defeating us.

I saw this dynamic play out when John and I were on safari as we followed a mother lion, her lion cub, and two lioness daughters. The group appeared to wander aimlessly through the tall autumn grass. Their stomachs were full, and I couldn't help noticing there was blood on their faces. They had just fed on a recent kill and appeared to be a bit sleepy. I saw a clump of trees in the distance, and I imagined they would head in that direction—but no! Right then they all plopped down on the side of the road not ten feet from our vehicle, cleaned up a bit, closed their golden eyes to the bright sun, and were all asleep in less than five minutes.

Here we were, a group of people with guns (okay, only the rangers had them) in a massive range roving vehicle, and the lions weren't the least bit impressed or troubled. It was time for their midmorning nap, and that was all there was to it.

LIVING IN THE LIGHT

Immediately I am struck with so many ideas and images of what living in the light might look like for us. For one, this captures the concept of living your life openly. Your windows and doors are open to welcome in light and family and friends. At our house the kitchen is always open because, with a house full of males, someone's mouth is always open. But there is nothing more critical to our health and survival than an open, light-filled heart.

Open up your lives. Live openly and expansively! (2 Corinthians 6:13)

This charge is so simple, so liberating, and yet at times so terrifying. We alone have the power to open our lives. First we open up, then we live openly, and then our life expands. Opening your life and living openly is a twofold process. You can *open your life* and yet not *live openly.* I know people who reveal a lot about themselves in certain areas of life and relationships, but if they were to live openly, more would be revealed that had previously been covered. Some people reveal one area in order to camouflage another.

Yet, as my mind plays over Paul's words, I find his charge almost irresistible. It makes me think of our lives as unwrapped gifts for our living God. Paul's wording paints images of lives open to receive all of what is revealed and released from above. Lives lived openly and on ever-expanding levels.

I want you to envision your life in motion—growing, strengthening, and expanding as you make contact with every facet of your immediate world.

You're out in the open now. The bright light of Christ makes your way plain. So no more stumbling around. Get on with it! The good, the right, the true—these are the actions appropriate for daylight hours. Figure out what will please Christ, and then do it. (Ephesians 5:8–10)

Do you hear this? Like the lioness, you are out in the open. There is no shadow realm of fear for you. There is no shameful, shaded place that can hold sway over your life. I love this call to action. The way is plain—get on with it!

So many people want to know what they are called to do. Well, let's not overcomplicate what God has made so simple. He calls us to do the good, the right, and the true. This is a list of acts that would not shame us if they came to the light of day. We are children of light called to daylight actions. We steer clear of the many activities that are conducted in the shadow realm. We figure out what is pleasing to God, and then we simply do it.

Our lives in Christ are like rays that continually expand and extend from that one stunning moment when his glorious light overtook our darkness. Each arrow could be likened to a ray of a sunburst of light and warmth exploding from that punctuated time.

I love it when the weather is fresh and warm enough to throw open the windows and air out my house. There is something exciting about a breeze sweeping through, removing the stale air as currents of freshness swirl through my domestic world. It brings a delicious wildness indoors, and the air in our home seems to expand as it catches life and movement laced with the fragrance of the out-of-doors. Fresh-cut grass, lilacs in bloom, pine resin, and the marvelous scent of a world cleansed by rain converge within the walls of a human habitation.

This dynamic of bringing the wild outside in is our reason for focusing so much attention on the lioness, for somehow she gracefully personifies the striking balance of ease and strength, rest and prowess, and the wild and safe, as does this scripture.

> Are you tired? Worn out? Burned out on religion? Come to me. *Get away with me and you'll recover your life. I'll show you how to take a real rest. Walk with me and work with me—watch how I do it. Learn the unforced rhythms of grace.* I won't lay anything heavy or ill-fitting on you. Keep company with me and you'll learn to live freely and lightly. (Matthew 11:28–30)

We who were raised as daughters of religion must again learn how to dance with God. Our children have a natural rhythm that John and I seem to have lost. Their response to music is freer than ours, because we were taught to repress all responses to music that was composed outside the church. This causes us to be rigid rather than responsive. The unforced rhythms of grace are the natural outflow and response to the supernatural working of God within our spirits.

Lovely ones, are you striving and exhausted as you work for him? Have you lost track of what it is to do life with him? Sometimes we all need this reminder. I know I do. Less than a year ago, I was on the edge of striving. Have you experienced that dangerous place where at any moment you might tip over and fall completely into a stress out? Well, you may not have, but I was there. I was worried about a meeting that was still three months away.

I openly shared my struggle with a friend, and she settled my anxiety with wise counsel. She encouraged me, saying that all I needed to do was bring my portion and our glorious Lord of the harvest would break it and cause it to multiply. I exhaled and remembered that he's been known to distribute what looks like little to the many.

Let's learn again how to live freely and lightly. Works and striving were our posture after the Fall, but rest should be our position after redemption.

> And that's not all: We throw open our doors to God and discover at
> the same moment that he has already thrown open his door to us.
> We find ourselves standing where we always hoped we might stand—
> out in the wide open spaces of God's grace and glory, standing tall
> and shouting our praise. (Romans 5:2)

I love this open invitation. For far too long, too many doors and windows have been shut by and to us. You and you alone, lovely one, have the power to open or close the entrances and windows of your life. You are the door-keeper with the power to choose what doors to open and shut. Boundaries are important, but God is safe to invite in. When you open the portals of your life to him, you discover you've arrived in a place of hope…released and open to God's grace and glory. In the following scripture, this reveal continues.

> We're not keeping secrets, we're telling them; we're not hiding things,
> we're bringing them out into the open. (Mark 4:22)

You're in on this. There is no secret of God's goodness being withheld from you. He has loved you with an everlasting love and invited you out with his loving-kindness. Just as God reveals his secrets, it is now safe for you to reveal yours. There is something so liberating in knowing that there is no secret sin, shame, or regulation that has sway over you. It is very empower-ing when you realize that God knows even the darkest secrets and broken rules and yet still openly declares his love for you.

In return, he asks that we would do the same. The God-entrusted message—God the Father is love, and his only begotten Son, Jesus, died to reconcile us—is too big and generous for us to keep it quiet. The gospel is not a secret. The mystery that awes is the why behind his message of love.

Who are we that our heavenly Father would be so mindful of us and give so glorious a gift? He revealed his loving plan and asked us to share it just as freely as we were welcomed in. Everyone deserves to hear of God's love.

As you read God's invitation to step into the open, perhaps you realized there is an area of your life that remains closed. It may be a closeted place of fear or dark shame. It may be a door or window you are afraid to open. I understand.

Often when our family travels, we request adjoining rooms. These rooms stand side by side, but two doors stand between them. Though access is available, there is no passage between the rooms until both doors are opened. John and I usually open our door immediately, and a little while later the boys open theirs after they have unpacked and changed their clothes. Once both doors are open, we have access to them, and they have access to us. And all of us can freely go in and out of the two rooms.

Lovely one, open the door. There's a light-filled room filled with family on the other side. Have no fear. God has not closed his door to you. Nor will a previously open door be shut in your face—his door is open. Simply open your side.

I am inviting you to open every painful area to him. Allow his life and light to chase away every hint of shadow.

The enemy of your soul wants you to remain in the shadows. Darkness complicates and confuses what is simple and obvious by light. Not only does our God want us to live in the light; he wants us to live light. You can walk unburdened, and it can happen right now. That is the beauty and power of prayer.

I have written some words to help you unlock and open your door, but feel free to allow your heart to be your guide.

Dear heavenly Father,

I come to you in the name of Jesus. Forgive me for hiding. I want to come into the light. I throw open any closed door, and I step into the light and goodness of your love. I embrace my right to be forgiven, and I choose to walk in truth because it alone establishes me in freedom. I am yours. I surrender to your love and will follow your ways. Light the path laid out before me. Amen.

NIGHT VISION

Now, sister of light, I can't wait to share with you another attribute I learned about the lioness. As you know, lionesses live in the light and hunt in the dark. But how is it that they manage these dark hunts? Is it their keen sense of smell or acute ability to hear? No!

Our lioness sisters can actually *see in the dark.*

How?

It appears the lioness and other members of the cat family have the unique ability to capture, refract, and then reflect light. They have the capacity to translate any light in their environment into vision. In complete darkness a lioness is just as blind as you and I would be. But if there is a glimmer of light punctuating the dark, it is caught and transformed into sight. Even the glow of the moon or the remote pinpricks of starlight enable the lioness's night vision.

Their pupils, which grant light entrance to the eyes, are different from ours. This gives them the ability to focus their vision when others cannot see. In a sense, the light they see by comes from within their eyes rather than from their environment. This is the reason a cat's eyes sometimes glow in the dark. They collect and reflect whatever light is available to them.

How can we do less? As the darkness of our world increases, we are going to have minimal environmental light to draw on. It is time we develop and focus the light source within.

> I could ask the darkness to hide me
>   and the light around me to become night—
> but even in darkness I cannot hide from you.
>   To you the night shines as bright as day.
> Darkness and light are the same to you. (Psalm 139:11–12, NLT)

If ever there was a time to capture this lioness skill of night vision, it's now. Most of us can see by day, but what I am proposing is that we develop our ability to see in the dark. The light lionesses see by is the light that is within their eyes. If we are lit from within, we will not be subject to the darkness of our environment. This will grant us improved vision with wider range and greater God-vantage.

God is light. In him there is no darkness. I wonder if we truly have space in our minds for this declaration. Where there is light, there is vision. Where there is vision, there is hope and recovery of sight. Where there is sight, there is revelation.

> God is not a hypothesis derived from logical assumptions, but an immediate insight, self-evident as light. He is not something to be sought in the darkness with the light of reason. He is the light.
>
> —ABRAHAM JOSHUA HESCHEL

I remember the very first scripture that was ever gifted to me in a letter. It came from Ephesians 1:

...that the God of our Lord Jesus Christ, the Father of glory, may give to you the spirit of wisdom and revelation in the knowledge of Him, *the eyes of your understanding being enlightened;* that you may know what is the hope of His calling. (verses 17–18, NKJV)

This phrase became a daily prayer. I whispered it as I closed my eyes each night and invited God into my dreams. By the light of day, I breathed its promise before I read Scripture. I found myself caught up in the wonder and promise of enlightened eyes with the capacity to see heaven played out in my earth.

What you behold, you become. What you see, you give expression to. I fear we have lost sight of just how vast is the wonder he has for us. *God, give us eyes to see.*

This request reveals what should be the pure, childlike simplicity of the prophetic. We hear it echoed in the directive of Eli to Samuel.

Go back and lie down. If the voice calls again, say, "Speak, GOD. I'm your servant, ready to listen." (1 Samuel 3:9)

The voice of God calls to the young Samuel when he is at rest and wakes him. Our response should mirror his: "Speak, God. I'm your servant, ready to listen."

Until Samuel answered and invited God to speak, he had only experienced the God who called him by name, but he had yet to speak in God's name.

How many of us have experienced only the God who calls us by name? Believe me, I am not belittling that experience, but it is just the beginning. Let's move on to the *something more* that each of us longs for. We long to know his counsel and work with him, which means allowing him to speak through us.

> GOD said to Samuel, "Listen carefully. I'm getting ready to do something in Israel that is going to shake everyone up and get their attention." (1 Samuel 3:11)

I have no doubt that even now God is saying to us, "Daughters, listen carefully. I'm going to do something in the earth that will shake things up and get the world's attention." God longs to have a people who will turn the world's attention to him.

In Samuel's day the voice of the Lord was rare, and the offerings of God's people and the honor of his worship were treated with contempt. Sexual sin was rampant...in the temple! The leader was unable or unwilling to restrain his sons because he inevitably benefited from his sons' violations.

In response, God turned away from the house of Eli and awakened a consecrated youth he could trust. The transgressions of our time are not so different, and God has children who are awakening and alive.

> But the boy Samuel was very much alive, growing up, blessed by GOD and popular with the people. (1 Samuel 2:26)

I have seen youth that look just like this—*very much alive,* blessed by God, and in favor with the people. The touch of heaven is on their lives, and God wants to position them alongside us, so together we will all do this.

For this to happen, there must be a prophetic awakening of eyes to see what God is doing, ears to hear what he is saying, and the ability to reveal his Word in such a vibrant and alive way that it removes the obstructions of the human heart.

In light of this I want to position these pages from a prophetic vantage. I want you to both expect and allow them to speak to the place of God-breathed wonder inside you. Know that as you read certain scriptures, images, and passages, they may evoke a stirring or quickening of the God-gift within.

It is the Holy Spirit enlarging the womb of your life and increasing your capacity to hear, see, and understand.

One time after I had finished speaking, a beautiful young woman whom God is anointing mightily came up to me and shared, "Every time I hear you speak, the baby within me stirs."

She was not expecting a child, at least not one as we know it. She was referring to the quickening of a God-something within her, and she didn't know how else to describe it.

Perhaps you've sensed the same stirring within you. In contrast, even now you argue, *I am not some prophet!* I'm a stay-at-home mother, a teenage girl, a busy career woman, or a grandmother. Maybe when you hear the word *prophet,* all that comes to mind is Jeremiah imprisoned with fire in his bones or Jonah in a whale's belly.

Well, I agree that your life looks very different from theirs. And perhaps you're not a prophet, but I would contend this doesn't mean you aren't prophetic.

To be prophetic is to be both visionary and farsighted, which gives you a strategic capacity to predict. Even our prayers take the form of prediction. We know he hears, therefore we know he answers and will show us great and mighty things we previously knew not of. We pray and look forward with expectation.

By the time Jesus walked the earth, the Pharisees had lost their sense of sight. The life and words of Jesus were a constant confrontation of their blindness, which enraged them. In John 5, Jesus had angered them again, but this time it was because he had healed on the Sabbath. This broke their Sabbath laws. But it is important to note that what Jesus did was in keeping with God's commandment, which instructed God's people to honor, remember, and keep the Sabbath holy.

What could be more holy than healing a crippled man? In their eyes it was holier to do nothing, or if a healing had to happen, at least do it on some other day of the week. Blinded by rules and regulations, they were tripping.

But Jesus defended himself. "My Father is working straight through, even on the Sabbath. So am I."

That really set them off. The Jews were now not only out to expose him; they were out to *kill* him. Not only was he breaking the Sabbath, but he was calling God his own Father, putting himself on a level with God.

So Jesus explained himself at length. "I'm telling you this straight. The Son can't independently do a thing, *only what he sees the Father doing. What the Father does, the Son does.* The Father loves the Son *and includes him in everything he is doing.* (John 5:17–20)

The Sabbath is not about our work; it is about resting in God's. Jesus's straight talk leaves us with some questions to answer.

First, are you God's daughter?

Do you want to see what your Father is doing?

Do you want to be included?

Do you want to be a light bearer or one who points out darkness?

Are you happy doing this Christian life independently?

Do you want to bring his wonder to a jaded, disillusioned, dying, and wounded world?

Jesus was never weird, but everywhere he went, he brought God-wonder.

If Jesus, the Son of God, could of himself do nothing, then we in and of ourselves can do nothing without the enlightened insight of the Holy Spirit. As he walked, so should we. We have the promise of his help. To underscore this, we are going to revisit Acts 2.

"In the Last Days," God says,
"I will pour out my Spirit
   on every kind of people:
Your sons will prophesy,
   also your daughters;
Your young men will see visions,
   your old men dream dreams.
When the time comes,
   I'll pour out my Spirit
On those who serve me, men and women both,
   and they'll prophesy.
I'll set wonders in the sky above
   and signs on the earth below,
Blood and fire and billowing smoke,
   the sun turning black and the moon blood-red,
Before the Day of the Lord arrives,
   the Day tremendous and marvelous;

And whoever calls out for help
   to me, God, will be saved." (Acts 2:17–21)

There is yet the promise of Wind Words in these last days. Believe me, at first glance I am wondering why God would choose us. As I travel our globe and look around, I think this is not the people or time period I would have chosen to pour out my Spirit upon. I would have picked a much nicer, cleaner, safer time when things were not so muddled and unclear.

I'd consider AD 50, right before they started killing the Christians, as an optimal choice. But then where would that leave us? Or maybe you are thinking you don't want or need a Spirit outpouring. Perhaps your church culture doesn't believe in one. But it really doesn't matter what I say or what you want. "In the Last Days," God says, "I will pour out my Spirit on every kind of people."

It sounds to me that in the end, he will have both a people and his say. That being said, what exactly does this mean? What might an outpouring of his Spirit look like? Well, let's explore and define the dynamic of a Spirit outpouring a bit further.

Approximately two thousand years ago, the Holy Spirit was released upon the earth to reveal Jesus and make new the hearts of believers near and far. So we have the Holy Spirit active in and among his body, the church. But I would be very hesitant to call what we have now an outpouring.

So what might an outpouring look like?

To explore this, we must first know the meaning of the word *spirit*. *Spirit* has four distinct meanings. The first is "strength." Under this definition we find the words *courage, character, will, force, fortitude, moral fiber, wisdom, determination, chutzpah, heart,* and *mettle.* The following scripture is an example of the Spirit poured out as courage and physical strength.

At that moment the Spirit of the LORD came powerfully upon him [Samson], and he ripped the lion's jaws apart with his bare hands. (Judges 14:6, NLT)

Okay, that's an intense example—not quite the dove-descending Spirit image.

An example of the Spirit as wisdom and moral fortitude would be this:

And the Spirit of the LORD will rest on him—
   the Spirit of wisdom and understanding,
the Spirit of counsel and might,
   the Spirit of knowledge and the fear of the LORD. (Isaiah 11:2, NLT)

And:

Create in me a clean heart, O God.
   Renew a loyal spirit within me. (Psalm 51:10, NLT)

Then there is the Spirit poured out as ability and skill:

I have filled him with the Spirit of God, giving him great wisdom, ability, and expertise in all kinds of crafts. (Exodus 31:3, NLT)

And last, here's a scripture that represents the Spirit as heart:

And I will give them singleness of heart and put a new spirit within them. I will take away their stony, stubborn heart and give them a tender, responsive heart. (Ezekiel 11:19, NLT)

Then there is the second main definition of *spirit,* and it is found beneath the word *soul.* Under this heading are the words *inner self, life force,* and *essence.*

> The human spirit can endure a sick body,
>   but who can bear a crushed spirit? (Proverbs 18:14, NLT)

> A glad heart makes a happy face;
>   a broken heart *crushes the spirit.* (Proverbs 15:13, NLT)

The next definition of spirit is "ghost, phantom, ghoul, and apparition." (I feel pretty sure this is not one we need to research any further.)

And last, spirit is defined as "a general feeling, attitude, mood, tendency, and atmosphere." You may have heard people say there's a good feeling or spirit in this place. They are not talking about a ghost or a dove. They are speaking of an atmosphere or an expectancy. More than likely in the upper room before the first outpouring, when the people were all in one accord and in one place, there was an atmosphere, mood, or spirit that welcomed and honored all that God would want to do.

> And wherever the Spirit of the Lord is, there is freedom. (2 Corinthians 3:17, NLT)

So here we see the Spirit fostering an atmosphere of freedom to receive from God.

You probably noticed I didn't define the *spirit* as the gift of tongues. Tongues are but one of the manifestations or evidences of the Holy Spirit's presence, but tongues are *not* the full expression of the Holy Spirit.

Throughout the Bible we've seen the Holy Spirit displayed in many of the ways just mentioned. The Spirit empowered Samson with superhuman strength so that he brought down a temple on the Philistines. Elijah outran the king's chariot. The courage of God came upon Gideon, and he rallied an army without weapons to defeat their oppressors. Through the power of the Spirit, Deborah, a lone woman in the desert, raised up a force for Israel's enemy oppressor to reckon with. By the power of the Spirit, Jesus displayed the character of God everywhere he went and to everyone he met.

And then there is us. The Bible says that in our day hearts will falter and fail because of fear. How will this debilitating fear be overcome? Maybe the answer is an outpouring of God-courage.

Because we are in a season of prophetic restoration, sometimes people can see what is on the horizon, but the repeating or telling of it feels contrived or forced. Some of you may have had encounters with a prophetic move in the past that seemed a bit weird or just plain wrong.

Well, let's be clear. God is after more than an office in the body or a group of people with titles. He is after people with his heart. We are prophetic merely by virtue of the time in which we were born. It is not because we've attended a seminar, but because, like Samuel, we attended our God. There's nothing wrong with a seminar; it is just that this is bigger than that.

God never meant it to be exclusive, elite, or limited. He meant creation and prophetic sights and sounds to open our eyes to see, our ears to hear, our mouths to speak, and our hearts to understand.

At the risk of oversimplifying the prophetic, I want to give you a few guidelines I gleaned by studying my favorite prophet, Isaiah. From the outset of his inspired and prophetic writings, we learn this:

He'll show us the way he works
so we can live the way we're made. (Isaiah 2:3)

171

I love this: the way he works is made known so we can live the way we were made to. We were made to live in sync with our God. He wants to reveal his ways and works to us. In light of this I found some basic visionary directives in Isaiah 49 that are echoed when Paul quotes Isaiah in Romans 9.

1. Look up.

2. Look around.

3. Look well.

4. Look ahead.

5. Tell the truth.

First, *look up.* If you are wondering how to lift your eyes to heaven, one needs to look no further than the book of Revelation to gain a heavenly perspective. Please don't think of this book as a scary end-times prophecy manual. It's a collection of revelations of the was, the is, and the is to come. God is independent of time; he is timeless, and he often speaks to us from this position. In college I took an entire semester on the book of Revelation, and I still am baffled by any human attempts to cram it into our time lines. I doubt John the revelator even understood all that he scribed. Sometimes it is okay not to know it all but to simply believe that there is a much grander drama going on behind the scenes than we can fathom.

There is an appalling need for an upward glance. We are still preaching Jesus walking on the shores of Galilee, hanging out with the guys, stripped of his deity, and moving around earth as the Son of Man. What about the Jesus who revealed himself to John? Picture this if you can:

The Son of Man,

in a robe and gold breastplate,

hair a blizzard of white,

Eyes pouring fire-blaze,
   both feet furnace-fired bronze,
His voice a cataract,
   right hand holding the Seven Stars,
His mouth a sharp-biting sword,
   his face a perigee sun.

I saw this and fainted dead at his feet. His right hand pulled me upright, his voice reassured me:

"Don't fear: I am First, I am Last, I'm Alive. I died, but I came to life, and my life is now forever. See these keys in my hand? They open and lock Death's doors, they open and lock Hell's gates. Now write down everything you see: things that are, things about to be. (Revelation 1:13–19)

Let's keep it real here. John was quite possibly the most stable of the Twelve. It appears he may have been one of Jesus's favorites. After all, he was the one Jesus confided in at the Last Supper. John saw Jesus revealed in heaven as the Son of God and fainted dead at his feet! This is a bit more than the lamb-carrying, fish-cooking Jesus. This is the Son of the Most High God revealed as a star-holding, armed, majestic warrior king. What if we started preaching this fierce revelation of Jesus? Seriously, look at the opening of the book of Revelation.

A revealing of Jesus, the Messiah. God gave it to make plain to his servants what is about to happen. He published and delivered it by Angel to his servant John. And John told everything he saw: God's Word—the witness of Jesus Christ!

How blessed the reader! How blessed the hearers and keepers of these oracle words, all the words written in this book!

Time is just about up. (Revelation 1:1–3)

This book is first and foremost an unveiling of Jesus. There is a blessing declared over the reader, hearer, and keeper of this revelation, so I am thinking it is more than worthy of our intention. Why would this reveal be necessary? Don't we have a record of how he lived and walked on this earth?

I believe it is a glimpse of who this triumphant Jesus, our Messiah, truly is. He stripped himself and became like us so we could strip ourselves and become like him. He is mighty, he is holy, he is glorious…so *look up*.

Next, there is the *look around*. Once we have glimpsed heaven's perspective, we begin to see ourselves, our surroundings, and the inhabitants of earth through a different or more enlightened set of eyes. Isaiah experienced this when he was undone by the revelation of God in Isaiah 6. He first saw his words as tainted. Then he thought of the people he lived with—tainted. A coal was used to purge his guilt and sin, and Isaiah responded with, "Send me." He was purged, enlarged, and ready to go to a people whom God told him ahead of time would not listen.

The contrasting, conflicting images of a holy, righteous God and what we see when we take our pulse and the pulse of the world around us should break our hearts. Look around you. Turn on the news or even a sitcom. What do you see? I see sin and injustice, but I also see children of light beginning to come out of hiding to face the gross darkness that amassed while they hid in the light.

Then, we are to *look well*. I believe this means we are to look for ways to make well or bring health to what is unwell and unhealthy in our world. This means shining light to expose areas of darkness, bringing hope to the hopeless near and far, turning from our wrong, and doing right. Restore health and strength to what is unhealthy or compromised. This could range from economic and educational solutions to relational issues.

All around us there are marriages and families that need their health restored. There are those in desperate need of medication, clean water, and food. There are the lonely to be set in families, orphans to be adopted, and captives to be rescued. There are oppressed and marginalized men and women to lift. *Look well.*

Now, to *look ahead* we will need the realization that our present choices live on and therefore require not only the insight of looking well but the foresight of looking ahead. We must live with deliberate intent of the see-through as we approach the intersections of life.

I have a Ninja motorcycle. It's probably not the smartest or the safest item I own, and in order for my husband to be comfortable with my driving something that dangerous, we took a motorcycle safety course. (I was the only female in our course.) In our classes we learned that most accidents happen at intersections, not because the motorcyclist is behaving dangerously, but simply because the drivers of the cars don't see them. In order to avoid an accident, we were taught a term to remind us to be proactive: SEE, which stands for search, evaluate, and execute.

When I approach an intersection on my Ninja, I am much more aware of the presence of the cars than those drivers are of me. Because of this coupling of my heightened awareness and their relative unawareness, I go into search mode. I scan the cars around and note who is talking on their phone, who is turning, who has noticed me, and who has not noticed me, and I also note the road conditions. Gravel and sand are not my friends. I search each intersection for potential problems and paths through to the other side.

Once my search is complete, I evaluate the conditions to determine my best approach. Sometimes when John and I are riding together, he will go first because his bike is so much louder, and they hear him coming. But if the traffic is all behind us, he wants me to go first so he has my back covered.

Then once the plan is set, we execute. We don't send mixed messages to the cars. I don't signal a left turn and then go straight. We make sure our intentions are as clear as we can communicate them.

Once in motion, I'm conscious of another lesson I learned on my Ninja: if you look down, you run the risk of going down. On a motorcycle, as in life, you need to look up and through the turns. You will complete the turn correctly if you keep your eyes on where you are headed (look ahead) rather than on where you've been or even where you are. Look toward the destination.

Where we are presently is not where we are headed. There is more ahead of us—more joy, more danger, more God, more evil, more justice, more freedom, more power, more light, more hope.

We're truly at an intersection between the way things are and the way they will or should be. This means there will be many unaware drivers navigating life around us. It is not their job to watch out for us; let's watch out for them.

And last, *tell the truth*. Paul said that Isaiah looked ahead and told the truth. In Isaiah's life, his words were not always received as truth. According to some historians, he was sawn in half for speaking the truth. It was not popular, well received, or convenient, but he not only spoke it; he lived out the truth he sent into the future.

It's who you are and the way you live that count before God. Your worship must engage your spirit in the pursuit of truth. That's the kind of people the Father is out looking for: those who are simply and honestly *themselves* before him in their worship. (John 4:23)

The following was Jesus's prayer for us.

Make them holy—consecrated—with the truth;
Your word is consecrating truth.
In the same way that you gave me a mission in the world,
I give them a mission in the world.
I'm consecrating myself for their sakes
So they'll be truth-consecrated in their mission. (John 17:17–19)

If we do not know what truth is, then we have God's Word to light our way to the realization of Jesus, who is the truth.

There are those who have looked up then failed to look around, so they hid. There are those who looked around but were overwhelmed because they never looked up, so they did nothing. There are those that looked ahead but failed to tell the truth, so they lived a lie. There are those who told the truth but never looked around, so the truth did not bring health to others.

So, in keeping with the hope of raising the bar in the next chapter, my goal is to scribe some wild wonder that we might recapture aspects of strength lost. Not by way of outpouring but by way of vision.

Please don't for a moment imagine that what I share with you on these pages was ever positioned weird. It wasn't. It was given to me in a revelation of wonder. This is my very human attempt to share with you a revelation bigger than my limited words can form.

Enlightened understanding is critical in a world of darkened foolishness. It is true—what you behold, you become. We must allow an inward vision and imagery of light to override our surroundings. It is time we look beyond the glaringly obvious and glimpse what God is doing in the midst of hopelessness.

Though we behold darkness, we are to declare light.

With eyes of understanding we will recover the wonder of just how vast our God is. God give us eyes to see.

As God's light increases, I believe there will be a divine prophetic awakening. God will give us eyes to see what he is doing, ears to hear what he is saying, and the boldness to speak his Word with authority. As this awakening happens, obstructions in the human heart will crumble.

Expect and allow God to speak his wonder deep within you. The prophetic ability to capture a glimpse of God-sight or vision is to behold his wonder and gain insight. Without this sight, life is at best a walk in the dark.

> If people can't see what God is doing,
>   they stumble all over themselves;
> But when they attend to what he reveals,
>   they are most blessed. (Proverbs 29:18)

Jesus was never weird, but everywhere he went he brought God-wonder. Why? He only did what he saw his Father doing. He simultaneously saw hurting humanity and his holy Father's response to it. He spoke light and truth to dispel the darkness and the lies of religion that had clouded the eyes of God's children and divided them from the living God.

Another term for *prophet* is *seer.* Jesus saw what others missed. He noticed the hurting and the outcast, and he touched the unclean. He didn't just see crowds; he saw people. He saw more than men and women—he saw individuals and hearts. Jesus saw light in the midst of darkness and exposed darkness that pretended to be light. He was the light of the world, and now you are to be that light bearer.

Go out into the world uncorrupted, a breath of fresh air in this
squalid and polluted society. Provide people with a glimpse of good
living and of the living God. Carry the light-giving Message into the
night. (Philippians 2:15)

There, lovely ones, is a description of our hunt in the dark. We live out
his light to the darkness. We let the lost and hurting world see into our transformed lives. We do not hide from darkness; rather we dispel it. Darkness
flees from our presence. As light approaches the realm of shadow, we discover what darkness has left behind. There are many who are hidden in dark
places waiting for the light of release.

It is time we hunt and rescue all who are yet captive and desperate for a
message of hope.

HUNTING IN THE DARK

Recently I had a chance to hunt in the dark as I searched in the shadowed
slums of India.

What I found in the dark surprised me. I went to Mumbai as the guest
of Life Outreach. They had formed an alliance with some on-site organizations that worked to rescue women and children trapped in the filth and
squalor of the slum brothels.

The Indian people are beautiful, and their culture can be both gracious
and kind, but the slums' conditions are deplorable. What I witnessed made
the environment of the movie *Slumdog Millionaire* look clean. Rats the size
of small cats slithered between the human and animal excrement, which
lined alleys and streets.

When I stepped out of the air-conditioned car that had navigated me safely through the insanity of Mumbai traffic, I was completely transported to a foreign world. Not foreign because it was in an exotic location, but foreign because it was a world of its own, a microculture of inhumanity.

It was monsoon season, and the combination of humidity and heat had elevated the stagnant air to stifling. Immediately I was assaulted by slum smells. A pungent combination of excrement and urine mingled with rotting food, filthy living conditions, and dirty people. The air itself felt heavy and oppressed by a dark spirit.

I sensed two elements in play—the beautiful Indian people and the brutal spirit that held them captive. In the slum there was no cloaking its effects or attributes. Men and women staggered under its weight as poverty, corruption, and depravity laid its heavy hand over all.

In an attempt to pass unnoticed, our team was outfitted in native Indian dress. But any illusion we had that this might work soon slipped away as we were noticed by all we passed.

Our pastor and missionary guides hurried us into their medical clinic. This clinic had built trust and earned the reputation of loving and serving the people. I stepped into the modest waiting room, where patients waited silently for the physician to see them. A ministry team made up of former madams awaited our arrival. We slipped into a side room where I was instructed that I was there to simply "bless" the women in the brothels.

Suddenly I knew the sermon in my backpack would be useless. I was out of my depth and keenly aware that Lisa the author and speaker would not cut it here. Because we were undercover, I couldn't use my Bible. My interpreter spoke limited English, and I spoke no Hindi. Connecting with these people could only be by God's Spirit.

To capture what we could of their stories, we taped a microphone inside my tunic and snaked the wire around my waist, anchoring the mike to a recorder taped to my pants. A hidden camera was disguised within the coils of the black scarf that encircled another woman's neck. We joined hands, prayed, and stepped out into the noisome streets.

I had an immediate sense of being watched. But this gaze felt more poignant than hostile. I looked up and across the street at a second-story window that framed the face of a beautiful Asian girl. I would have guessed her to be no more than fifteen years old. Her young face displayed a mixture of hurt and hopelessness. Only then did I realize she was behind bars, locked in a brothel.

How do you answer such a look?

A smile can't be shared. I couldn't shake my head and risk the perception that my reaction to *her* was judgment or disgust. I held her gaze until she looked away. When I looked down, I saw a stairwell. At its base sat an angry knot of men. They met my gaze with open disdain as if to say, "Who do you think you are? Get out. You don't belong here!"

No doubt I did not. No human made in the image of God belonged in such an awful place. This was not a place to belong—it was a place to escape from.

One of the women sensed my angst and threw her arm around my waist. "Come! I will help you cross the street!" She herded me through the people, bicycles, and cars, which traveled muddy roads without rules or lanes.

After a day in the slum, I learned the only pedestrian rule was don't stop once you've started crossing a street. You walk on fearlessly no matter how many bikes, motorcycles, and cars are headed in your direction. Once I hesitated in the middle of the road, and two former madams flanked me and pushed me on across as they shook their heads. "No stopping! We protect you." And they did.

The first brothel we came to had a common area of no more than five feet by eight feet. This was where clients waited for girls to service them. It was also where the women gathered to cook, socialize, and tend to their children. From the shadowed room they could observe the squalor of the street outside their door. In this enclave a number of broken women had gathered to hear of God's love.

I entered and couldn't help but notice another door. It was slightly draped and led to a narrow hallway lined with rows of what looked like bathroom stalls. I later learned this was where the girls slept and serviced their clients. Looking down this hall, I noted a few doors were closed, which could mean a girl was resting or occupied.

I turned my attention to the women before me. They covered the floor and the benchlike seating area that lined both sides of the room. They huddled under veils and peered doubtfully at us as we filed in.

The interpreter greeted them in Hindi. They listened intently and respectfully nodded in their unique side-to-side Indian fashion.

It wasn't long before I heard my name in the mix of Hindi words. Heads turned in my direction. I flashed a look of desperation toward the pastor. He responded with a lifting motion of his arms and repeated his earlier admonishment: "Bless them… They've been waiting for you…here like this for two hours!"

I introduced myself and shared where I was from. I told them I had four sons and a grandson on the way. My words sounded empty and hollow to my own ears. What could my frame of reference mean to these women? All they knew flew in the face of my American "normal." But they were polite and nodded mildly.

I shared how we'd traveled a great distance to let them know they were not alone. Women the world over had them in their hearts and wept over their plight.

What was this? They were not alone? Word of their despair had escaped the slums? Others had cried over their loss? I shared how many women carried these hidden daughters of India before the throne of God in prayer. Their faces began to shine with silent tears.

Sometimes I wonder if we truly understand the power in the realization of a connection. We are not alone in our struggles. We are not alone in our hopes. Jesus promised to be with us always.

I confessed my personal regret. How, in my youth, I'd squandered the very sexual purity and dignity that had been forcefully stolen from them. I had chosen promiscuity but later opened the door to God, and his love had flooded my life and saved me from destruction. They leaned in.

I sensed the Holy Spirit as he highlighted each and every woman. They were not a collection of women; they were individual daughters. I touched each of their faces in turn and trusted God would likewise stretch forth his hand and punctuate my human words by his Spirit. As I made contact, I gently declared, "God has a plan for your life."

Tears traced their upturned cheeks at this mention of a God who'd sought them out and visited them in their captive darkness. They intimately knew what it meant to live under the oppression and schemes of another. Each girl was living in a nightmare someone else had planned for her life. Every one of the women I interviewed had been abducted or tricked into a life of sexual slavery. They had been taken captive by the promise of the very thing I now offered—hope.

Each had dared to hope for something more—a better job, an education, or just to be loved. Some hoped to escape the cruel poverty of their villages.

These women had been lied to by men and women they had once trusted. There were stories of uncles, husbands, brothers, cousins, aunts, and even friends who had sold them. Their dream of a better life was used to betray them. I asked them to hope again, to trust Jesus, the Son of God, who could not lie.

I said other things to them as well. Things I've now forgotten. Phrases and words, which if repeated on these pages, might sound infantile or remedial in our Western society. But in the moment they were heaven breathed.

Without any fanfare, an atmosphere of heaven invaded the cramped area. A connection had been made when they responded to the living God, who offered hope to every one of them.

Sensing this shift and my inadequacy to communicate, I turned to the pastor. He prayed with and for these women. As he called upon heaven, the women in our group moved in among these precious daughters and embraced each one, surrounding them likewise in prayer. In that moment it felt as though the walls moved back.

I noticed a customer as he exited, zipping his pants and casting a look of disgust over his shoulder as he went. We were unusual visitors.

FOCUSED AND FIERCE

Consider the following scripture:

> I dare to believe that the luckless
>   will get lucky someday in you.
> You won't let them down:
>   orphans won't be orphans forever.

Break the wicked right arms,
    break all the evil left arms.
Search and destroy
    every sign of crime.
GOD's grace and order wins;
    godlessness loses.

The victim's faint pulse picks up;
    the hearts of the hopeless pump red blood
    as you put your ear to their lips.
Orphans get parents,
    the homeless get homes.
The reign of terror is over,
    the rule of the gang lords is ended. (Psalm 10:14–18)

Can you really hear this? It includes every element we need to hunt in the dark: belief, justice, triumph, healing, hope, adoption, restoration, righteousness, an end, and a new beginning! Now is the time to pray these words, and if we send out God's Word, he will watch over it.

This is an extreme-measure, mafia-type prayer. Personally I am wearied and tired of safe, nice prayers. "Break both their arms and disable them, God" is a dangerous prayer. It is an intense petition. And I can't imagine praying this one quietly or passively. Psalm 10 is actually God's promise that I took as a sword when I traveled recently to Southeast Asia. Every time I saw injustice, I wielded it.

Be focused and fierce in prayer. Close your eyes to the obvious, and behold a vision of restoration and justice. This is what God wants to bring to earth. There are people who need you to close your eyes and see them when you pray. I mean really pray tenacious prayers that reach heaven and scare you as they pass over your lips.

A passive church will not endure. The best hope for the church is that we will hunt in the dark until the Prince of Peace comes and ends this reign of terror. For this to happen, we must individually and collectively seek, search, and recover what is now hidden.

Believe me, you do not have to travel to India to find desperate people trapped in the dark. There are captive men, women, and children everywhere. They wait for us to step out and step up. To open the door to freedom and move away from any areas of personal darkness so we can bring them into light.

When we are filled with God's light, we will truly extract the lost from darkness. This is not the time to fight over doctrine or to compete for megaministry or church status. We should be serving rather than power positioning and comparing ourselves.

Wake up! Orphans are waiting for adoption and care on every level. Thousands of lonely, isolated individuals are praying and hoping that despite all appearances they are not alone.

I've painted the concept of the "hunt in the dark" on a large, international scale as I shared on these pages the story of pain and trafficking in India, but let it serve for perspective. With this insight do not imagine your pain or the pain of those near you is inconsequential. God is near to all who are hurting. The agony of captivity, isolation, betrayal, violation, abuse, and hopelessness visits the people of every nation. People have the same needs everywhere, but not all people have the same resources.

Let us be faithful stewards and multiply our prosperity well. You are blessed to bless others. Countless places need the blessing you can bring. You don't have to go far away to give. Hopelessness may be found in your workplace or where you shop. Abuse might be happening in the marriage of a friend. Isolation may be rampant among the people with whom you worship. Your children may feel betrayed by someone at their school.

Often the very act of setting hope in motion for others becomes our healing. People the world over need the love and value that Jesus the Christ adds to the human soul. Whether they cower in corners of overwhelming poverty, sit in ivory towers, or rest uneasily in a house of cards, the lines have been drawn, the boundaries have been set. There is life, and there is death and destruction. There is hope, and there is despair. There is light, and there is darkness. The realms have never been more clear, and the stakes have never been higher.

Lionesses live in the light and hunt in the dark. So, brave ones, I can't imagine a better example of how we should conduct ourselves. I believe you hold this book in your hands because you are a daughter of promise. You've thrown wide the door. Now learn to live and rest in his glorious light. Let's also live lightly together; don't allow care or worry to isolate or overwhelm you.

Let's open wide our eyes and learn to see in the dark—to look beyond and see hearts and the things that are hidden. Together let's hunt in the dark and bring others into God's light. Like the lioness, let's strike the balance between relaxed and open and intense and fierce. Rest in him, relax with one another, and together be ferocious in the face of darkness.

Walking with a Lion

Stop weeping! Look, the Lion of the tribe of
Judah, the heir to David's throne, has won
the victory.

REVELATION 5:5, NLT

It's common to feel as if you are walking alone through challenging situations. But in actuality, something hidden yet powerful is walking ahead of you, leading the way. As you read on, you may realize you've walked with our Lion, Jesus the Christ, unaware.

Sometimes, following can be frightening. Our challenge isn't necessarily in understanding what God tells us to do—it lies in how to do it. Most people desperately want to be on track with God but have no idea how.

Jesus gave what initially appeared to be a simple directive. Look at these two different versions of Matthew 16:24.

If anyone desires to come after Me, let him deny himself, and take up his cross, and follow Me. (NKJV)

And for more clarity…

Anyone who intends to come with me has to let me lead. You're not in the driver's seat; I am. Don't run from suffering; embrace it. Follow me and I'll show you how. (The Message)

The directive is clear—deny yourself, take up your cross, and follow. But it is the how that presents the challenge.
How do you deny yourself?
What is it to take up a cross?
How do you follow someone you cannot see?
The answer is simple: Jesus leads…we follow.

WALKING BY FAITH

I frequently have the opportunity to address gatherings of young girls in question-and-answer forums. I'm surprised how many times I answer a question only to hear "But how?"
How do you know when God is speaking?
How can I forgive my father?
How did you get free from an eating disorder?
How do you know when a guy is the right one?
How did you get over your fear, shame, guilt?
When I faced the struggles these girls were asking about, I simply believed

God's Word was true and then followed where it led me. Jesus is the Word made flesh. As we read God's Word, we see how he walked and where he leads. Most people who have been led to complete difficult courses did not initially see themselves as able. But they gathered their courage and followed Jesus in faith.

> Through acts of faith, they toppled kingdoms, made justice work,
> took the promises for themselves. (Hebrews 11:33)

Because people acted in faith, corrupt kingdoms were overthrown, wrongdoing was met with justice, and God's promises became real. We enter into God's plan and promise in and for our lives by faith. It takes faith to follow where our Lion leads.

Faith overrides doubt. We ask God, "Are you there? I can't feel you." By faith we hear our Lion answer, "I will never leave you or forsake you" (Hebrews 13:5, NKJV).

Faith lends expectancy when we pray. A prayer offered in faith will heal the sick, and the Lord will make you well. And if you have committed any sins, you will be forgiven (see James 5:14).

What is an act of faith?

For Abraham, our father of faith, it meant following God on a walk through the wilderness even though he had no idea where he would end up. As I read about Abraham and Sarah's journey, I noticed God gave them the land they had passed through as well as the land they could see.

> By an act of faith, Abraham said yes to God's call to travel to an
> unknown place that would become his home. When he left he had
> no idea where he was going. (Hebrews 11:8)

If Sarah and Abraham had remained in Ur—where everything was comfortable and familiar—they would not have inherited God's promise.

Oh how difficult it is for us to walk by faith. We want a map, but instead God weaves us a mystery.

This sojourn of faith develops something courageous in us. Set before each of us is an obstacle course full of great adventure and the surety that our Lion will not lead us on a path that he himself has not paced. Whenever God calls us to something we haven't seen or done before, it's daunting. At times God leads us to follow an inclination or direction that no one has dreamed of treading before. All we have is a challenge and his invitation: "Daughter, will you follow me…even if you're afraid?"

Not long ago a friend called me to share something she was invited to do that looked at once frightening and strategic. She had been asked to participate on a panel of males who were addressing a large gathering of highly influential male leaders. Even her husband challenged her involvement, wondering why they had asked her.

She called me because the conference brochure had just arrived, and after seeing her own face as the only female speaker, she felt overwhelmed and afraid that she was in over her head.

Before I knew what I was saying, I blurted out, "You have been preparing your whole life for this moment. You are well able to do this and do it well. You will do this in an attractive, godly, irresistibly wise way."

I heard her exhale slowly and sensed her nodding. I knew she wouldn't be facing this challenge alone. A Lion would stand beside her. She'd follow him and stay her course, perhaps trembling, but with the knowledge that she was not alone.

Those who follow Jesus keep the company of a Lion. Jesus is our Lamb that was slain and rose again as the Lion of Judah.

The Lion from Tribe Judah, the Root of David's Tree, has conquered. (Revelation 5:5)

DON'T HOLD BACK

In order to put some fear and trembling back into your Christian devotion, I want you to picture yourself walking in the company of a lion. Who knows? God just might ask you to do something frightening.

You see, picturing Jesus as he was when he walked along the Sea of Galilee and taught on the mount is not vast enough to capture who he is now. The Son of God visited this earth as a man, stripped of his divine privileges. But he no longer walks the earth clothed in humanity, except in the form of his sons and daughters. He is seated on high, part of a wild, extravagant, heavenly pageantry—the very image of strength and splendor.

Lift your eyes and see him now as the Lion of Judah, resplendent in majesty and strength. He wants you to live in a place of amazement and wonder, not in a domain of rules and duty. Allow his voice to stir something profoundly untamed and deeply wild within you! God's promises to the young Jeremiah are his promises to you, his fearless, prophetic daughter:

"Before I shaped you in the womb,
   I knew all about you.
Before you saw the light of day,
   I had holy plans for you:
A prophet to the nations—
   that's what I had in mind for you."

But I said, "Hold it, Master GOD! Look at me.
  I don't know anything. I'm only a boy!"

GOD told me, "Don't say, 'I'm only a boy.'
  I'll tell you where to go and you'll go there.
I'll tell you what to say and you'll say it.
  Don't be afraid of a soul.
I'll be right there, looking after you." (Jeremiah 1:5–9)

Like Jeremiah, in order for you to be effective, you must be settled in the reality that God is right there with you. This postures you not to fear, no matter what others say or do.

Your journey through life is accompanied by many voices and influences. Some strengthen and undergird your direction; others sway and deter you from your path. Some voices spur you on to places yet unknown, and others hold you back. There are voices from your past—voices of family, voices of disappointment, and voices of fear—that intermittently yell and whisper, "Turn aside! Turn back. You might fail. You might get hurt." These voices urge you to protect yourself.

Amid these negative, life-draining voices is the call of powerful, life-giving voices. They are always present, but if you choose not to listen for them, you might miss them. The voices of the heavenly host who went before call out through the Scriptures, cheering you forward and onward, "Don't listen to your fears or the terror of those around you. Don't listen to the lies of your enemy who is condemned and tormented. Don't be distracted. We need you! Stay your course and run your race!"

Remember, in the presence of a lion, all lesser beasts tremble. While Satan is said to be *like* a lion who roams the earth seeking someone to devour (see 1 Peter 5:8, NLT), he is *not* a lion. He just mimics one. Satan is no match for our true Lion. The dark lord and his cohorts masquerade as those who divinely roar, but his companions are shades and shadows that must borrow light and God's creative genius.

TRUST YOUR LION ENCOUNTERS

When I was a young girl, I was given the entire set of The Chronicles of Narnia as a Christmas gift. Each title was like buried treasure. When I finished the series, I cried. Not just because the stories were over, but because I'd lost my connection with a marvelous and otherworldly place. I understood Aslan represented Jesus, but I could not reconcile the Jesus I had been introduced to with the wild, untamed, yet touchable lion I had grown to love in the Chronicles.

He walked among his children. I did not want to return to silent, haloed icons and cold holy water. I wanted the living, breathing lion back. I wanted an encounter with God so profound, warm, and alive that his tangible existence was undeniable. I wanted a love so powerful it frightened me. I wanted justice so pure it took my breath away.

I wanted to be Lucy in a world where animals and trees talked. Where virtue and truth were rewarded. Where mistakes were forgiven without penance.

God invites us to come before him with childlike, wide-eyed innocence and embrace the wonder of his love and redemption. But the regulations of religion and the passage of time caused many of us to stray. And we lost sight of the Lion of our youth.

With this concept in mind, let's visit Lucy on the pages of *Prince Caspian,* the fourth book in the Narnia series. As we join them, the children are exhausted, lost, and about to take yet another wrong turn when Lucy sees Aslan, her Lion.

"Look! Look! Look!" cried Lucy.

"Where? What?" asked everyone.

"The Lion," said Lucy. "Aslan himself. Didn't you see?" Her face had changed completely and her eyes shone.

"Do you really mean—?" began Peter.

"Where did you think you saw him?" asked Susan.

"Don't talk like a grown-up," said Lucy, stamping her foot. "I didn't *think* I saw him. I saw him."

"Where, Lu?" asked Peter.

"Right up there between those mountain ashes. No, this side of the gorge. And up, not down. Just the opposite of the way you want to go. And he wanted us to go where he was—up there."

"How do you know that was what he wanted?" asked Edmund.

"He—I—I—just know," said Lucy, "by his face."

The others just looked at each other in puzzled silence.[1]

When the Lion appears, your countenance reflects it. With vision comes a knowing.

I remember seeing this *knowing* on Addison's face when he told me he believed Julianna was his future bride. I'd just arrived home from a women's conference in Kiev, and in the short span of my absence (six days), my son had met the love of his life. He wanted me to join them for lunch that very day. We sat on the deck, and I listened as he told me he knew she was "the one."

When I asked him how he knew this, he held my gaze and explained, "I just *know.*" In that moment I knew too. I recognized that my son had seen something more in this young woman, something that gave him strength to follow a path he could not explain. As his mother, I would support him on this journey. Before I even spent time with Julianna, I believed she was the one for my son, even if I didn't yet understand.

When we have these Lion encounters, we should trust this knowing, even if others miss what is obvious to us. Despite the skepticism of the other children, Lucy trusted what she had seen and knew to be true.

After Lucy tells them the direction Aslan wants them to go, the other children question her. They not only doubt whether or not she has seen Aslan; they wonder why he appeared to her. They decide to vote whether to follow Lucy and her Lion or take a more direct route. Lucy loses, and the children turn and take another path. She follows the group, crying as they pursue an opposite course.

I think we all know how she felt.

When you see a lion, or a God-sign, that others don't see, there will be questions. They'll want to know why you were shown something they missed. I've learned that God alone can answer this question. He can do as he pleases. God reveals himself in different ways to different people. This dynamic should create interdependence throughout the body of Christ rather than raise questions. If each of us has a portion, leaders will strengthen and challenge one another. It's awful to be misunderstood and then led in the wrong direction. It feels horrible when those around you don't value your God-given insight. Remember, even in this, God is working toward a bigger purpose. Don't allow rejection and misunderstanding to introduce judgment or bitterness to your soul. Process it.

Returning to *Prince Caspian*—after a day filled with many wrong turns and an almost fatal encounter, the children end up back where they had started. Sore and exhausted, they drop off to sleep. Aslan knows Lucy is hurting, and in order to prevent further damage, he visits her again.

From the shadows outside their camp, Aslan calls to Lucy, who is strangely awake after such a trying day. Excited by his voice and overcome with joy, she goes to him. In the process of describing her day, Lucy criticizes her brothers and sister for not following her advice. From deep within the Lion comes the "suggestion of a growl." Startled, Lucy asks him if she has done something wrong.

"But it wasn't my fault anyway, was it?"

The Lion looked straight into her eyes.

"Oh, Aslan," said Lucy.... "I couldn't have left the others and come up to you alone, how could I?..."

Aslan said nothing.[2]

The Lion looked straight into her eyes. What is it about the presence of God that brings such clarity to our distorted human vision? I've often gone into his presence, thinking I am a victim who has been misunderstood and maligned, only to realize certain choices were mine alone. Yet in our Lion's presence, I don't feel ashamed. I feel empowered, positioned, and prepared to move forward.

At one time or another, we all find ourselves in just such a hard place. You had a God-inclination to go one way and pressure from peers or family to pursue another. Maybe you were tempted to compromise your faith or morals by just going along with the pack and remaining quiet. Regardless of pressure, you have noticed when you go to our Lion, excuses don't fly. They are met with silence. I have often heard that if God is silent, revisit what he last told you to do. Did you accept it, do it, say it, or give it? If not, he is still waiting for your response.

"You Are a Lioness..."

God does not change his directives just because humans take a vote or disagree with him. He also doesn't play the blame game. He waits and listens until we have moved from accusation to honesty. This posture of humility empowers us to arise and walk with him into the wild.

C. S. Lewis captured this profound truth so well in the following interaction between Lucy and Aslan. Lucy has realized she should have followed Aslan, even if the others didn't join her. With this revelation comes a new responsibility. Aslan gives her another chance and asks her to wake her brothers and sister, tell them she has seen him again, and it's time to follow.

> "But they won't believe me!" said Lucy.
>
> "It doesn't matter," said Aslan.
>
> "Oh dear, oh dear," said Lucy. "And I was so pleased at finding you again.... And I thought you'd come roaring in and frighten all the enemies away—like last time. And now everything is going to be horrid."
>
> "It is hard for you, little one," said Aslan. "But things never happen the same way twice."

Let's pause a moment. I love this picture of the human response to a God-directive. He sets us up for an adventure, and we imagine it will be a "horrid" failure. Lucy goes from hopeful to hiding.

Let's continue:

Lucy buried her head in his mane to hide from his face. But there must have been magic in his mane. She could feel lion-strength going into her. Quite suddenly she sat up.

"I'm sorry, Aslan," she said. "I'm ready now."

"Now you are a lioness," said Aslan. "And now all Narnia will be renewed."[3]

When I read the declaration, I was overcome. "Now you are a lioness…" I believe God wants to make this same declaration over each of his daughters as we sit up, stop crying, and make ourselves ready. Then God can proclaim, "Now you are courageous. Now you have my perspective. You realize your strengths. You are fit for battle." Remember, you are part of an army engaged in an all-out battle.

The Courage to Make a Difference

And what of this battle? It seems darkness grows as our light flickers.

It's time to announce that a lion is in our midst. Perhaps we missed him while we bickered about the unimportant. Our ranks have become divided and our focus distracted as the powers of darkness have caused havoc on the earth we are charged to keep. A battle rages around us, but we are too busy fighting within our camp.

Now to the King eternal, immortal, invisible, the only God, be honor and glory for ever and ever. Amen. Timothy, my son, I give you this instruction in keeping with the prophecies once made about you, so that by following them you may fight the good fight, holding on to faith and a good conscience. Some have rejected these and so have shipwrecked their faith. (1 Timothy 1:17–19, NIV)

There are promises thrown into our future. We wage war with weapons of light and hope. He is not defeating death again. He has won that victory. But it is time we walk out his triumph and encourage others to follow.

Even now our nation is on the verge of moral, economic, and spiritual collapse. We are beset with enemies and terrorists throughout the world and within our borders. Fear and treachery sow their discord on every front, and there are those among us who imagine we cannot think for ourselves.

In my opinion, our current climate is similar to England's a few hundred years ago. An empire was born from a torn and tattered land, and Great Britain's people were renewed when a young woman awoke a lioness.

At twenty-five years of age, Queen Elizabeth I took the throne of a country that was financially and morally bankrupt. England was threatened on all sides by stronger nations that were united by Catholicism. In contrast, England was split by the religious wars that raged within its borders. Great Britain faltered in the aftermath of the tumultuous reigns of King Henry VIII and Queen Mary.

Yet, listen to Queen Elizabeth's coronation speech: "The burden that has fallen upon me maketh me amazed."[4] Centuries later I find her words timely and provocative. What kind of woman chooses to be amazed by an enormous burden?

I'm glad this queen didn't excuse herself as too young, too frail, or the wrong gender. Her right to the throne was repeatedly challenged. But even when she was referred to as the bastard daughter of King Henry VIII, she did not relent. Instead, she chose to be amazed. Her astonishment moved her into the realm of awe, wonder, and dependence on God.

Early on, Elizabeth had learned to choose her words carefully. If she hadn't, she would not have lived to age twenty-five. From birth to grave, she was surrounded by those who wished her harm. In her court and country lived traitors and usurpers who would have loved to trap her in her words. Her half sister Mary, who was queen before her, earned the title "Bloody Mary" because of the number of executions during her reign. Mary looked for opportunities to kill Elizabeth and went as far as imprisoning her in the Tower of London, where Elizabeth's mother, Anne Boleyn, had been imprisoned before she was beheaded. Queen Mary's attacks and conspiracies against Elizabeth only ended with her death.

Shortly after Elizabeth became queen, her cousin Mary, Queen of Scots, who was backed by the Catholic Church, returned to Great Britain and repeatedly tried to steal the throne of England. In the end Elizabeth had her executed when a blatant assassination attempt came to light. Elizabeth was betrayed, rejected, and mistrusted, but she allowed hardship to fashion her into the best ruler England has ever known.

Rather than marry and produce an heir, Queen Elizabeth I pledged to be both bride and mother to her realm. This overwhelming level of commitment freed her to focus on the strategies that established her kingdom in strength. In addition to constantly educating and improving herself, she surrounded herself with wise counsel and kept close tabs on the tone and welfare of her subjects.

Under Queen Elizabeth's reign,

- religious factions were united under the Church of England;

- England's economy went from solitary and dependent to diversified and independent;
- science and the arts flourished;
- England became a naval force;
- the settlement and exploration of America thrived.

Queen Elizabeth brought her country into the Golden Age and turned a small kingdom into an empire.

No wonder she has been called a lioness. Even with all these accomplishments, her role as queen never ceased to be a burden. She said,

> To be a king and wear a crown is a thing more glorious to them that see it than it is pleasant to them that bear it.[5]

As history books tell us, she did more than bear a crown; she pioneered innovation, trade, and exploration. She understood the strength behind an undivided allegiance and nurtured a national evolution, even as countries such as France were poised to be torn apart by revolution.

Elizabeth was fearless on the battlefield. Here is an excerpt of her speech as she prepared to ride into battle with her troops.

> Let tyrants fear, I have always so behaved myself that under God I have placed my chiefest strength and safeguard in the loyal hearts and good will of my subjects. And therefore I am come amongst you as you see at this time not for my recreation and disport, but being resolved in the midst and heat of the battle to live or die amongst you all. To lay down for God and for my kingdom and for my people my honour and my blood even in the dust....

I know I have the body of a weak and feeble woman but I have the heart and stomach of a King, and of a King of England too, and think foul scorn that Parma or Spain or any Prince of Europe should dare invade the borders of my Realm to which rather than any dishonour shall grow by me, I myself will take up arms.... We shall shortly have a famous victory over those enemies of God, my Kingdom and of my People.[6]

And they did.

Do you see what happened when one woman chose to be amazed rather than terrified? Elizabeth followed God fearlessly, attentive to her destiny. She was not casual in her pursuit of God's counsel and kept prayer journals in three different languages. The results are nothing short of astonishing. Perhaps you feel God is calling you to something extraordinary or frightening. If so, allow the examples of Lucy and Queen Elizabeth I to encourage you forward.

It doesn't matter what others see for you. If God has spoken, believe him. Go where he tells you to go; listen to what he speaks to you. Follow this lion as he leads, and trust the "knowing" even when others might not understand.

Are you ready to be amazed?

From a Whisper to a Roar

I was not the lion, but it fell to me to give the lion's roar.

WINSTON CHURCHILL

Lions roar.

No doubt you know this. But did you know lionesses roar as well?

In order for lions or lionesses to roar effectively, they must first change their posture. The unleashing of such a raw declaration of might requires a bow. Their powerful heads drop, and they expand their chests in order to fill their lungs with air. I wonder if they feel ready to burst as they let go a declaration, which has been known to travel five miles on the still night air and shake the hearts of men and creatures in its path. A lion's roar can surround you and stop you in your tracks with its fearsome wonder.

Likewise, if we, the lionesses of God, are ever going to produce a sound of such magnitude, it will require a change in our present posture. To have the ability to roar, we must drop our high-held heads and bow. This stance of humility and prayer will position us to receive a fresh infilling of the breath of God's Spirit. I believe this roar will happen as our intake of God's Spirit exceeds our capacity to contain his fullness of life. When we can no longer hold back his truth, love, and goodness, we'll release a stirring declaration of all God is.

But unlike the roar of the lioness, our roar will be more than merely sound. Our declaration will be a divine merging of arresting words, deeds, and acts of faith. When all the intangibles of faith, hope, and love become tangible in individuals and expressed in our unified response to the world's needs and God's love, our roar will be heard. As we exemplify our Lion, the world will hear his roar. Then all lesser lords and noises will be arrested, and a cry will arise, "Worship God alone!"

Our world is filled with roars. As I explored the concept of the roar, I discovered so many things that are capable of roaring. Oceans roar. The wild, unleashed wind roars. Waterfalls roar as they tumble in vast volumes from great heights. Excited fans crowded into athletic arenas roar.

The four living creatures before the throne of heaven roar, "Holy, Holy, Holy," and the sound of this roar shakes the very doorposts of heaven's architecture (Isaiah 6:4). On earth we repeat their words in the form of songs, but this declaration of the Holy God originated as a roar.

Our God Most High, the Lord of all...roars.

> God roars like a lion from high heaven;
> thunder rolls out from his holy dwelling— (Jeremiah 25:30)

And again,

> I'm The Holy One and I'm here—in your very midst.

"The people will end up following GOD.

    I will roar like a lion—

Oh, how I'll roar!

    My frightened children will come running from the west."

        (Hosea 11:9–10)

What magnifies an utterance so that it is more than a whisper, growl, cry, or shout? Does volume alone make it a full-on roar that awes with power?

IT BEGINS WITH A WHISPER

To answer, let's first explore the dynamic of a whisper.

The psalmist wrote:

> I hear this most gentle whisper from One
> I never guessed would speak to me. (Psalm 81:5)

Here the psalmist explained his wonder at experiencing God's whisper. Hadn't he scribed and sung his allegiance to God? Perhaps in this psalm he is revisiting the wonder of when his communion with God began. We do not recognize what we haven't heard before. David first heard God whisper as a young shepherd, and afterward he heard God's voice everywhere. God's voice is described as the "most gentle whisper." The Magnificent One speaks in tender undertones, underscoring the harsh reality of our human life.

And thus our invitation to be quiet: "Be still, and know that I am God!" (Psalm 46:10, NLT)

I am certain that God the Most High and Creator of all things knew his children would be arrested and calmed by his very whisper.

I find the idea of a God who whispers more surprising than a God who shouts. You can expect a thunderous voice from a God so vast, but a whisper is unexpected. With this gentle reverberation, God has the ability to bring focus. Just as deep calls to deep, a God-whisper is the echo of the Creator resounding within his children, the created.

Elijah looked for God in the wind, the earthquake, and the fire, but he heard him in the whisper (see 1 Kings 19:12). When Elijah heard the still, small voice, he stepped out of his cave and listened to what God told him.

Hushed tones carry profound and intimate pronouncements to those who will quiet themselves enough to hear. In this stillness our spirit hears the adoptive whisper of a Father. Each of us longs to hear God's whisper. You were created to hear your Creator. Allow him to speak into the depths of your soul and fulfill the longing of your heart.

I believe that when God speaks, it always begins as a whisper. Everything out loud starts with a whisper. When I was pregnant and felt life quicken within me, it was a whisper of the child to come. A cry begins with a whisper within. Perhaps you first heard a God-whisper in response to a cry from within your soul. "God, I am hungry, frightened, and alone."

He whispered back, "Don't be afraid. I am here, child."

Sometimes I even imagine women as whispers. A mother rocking her frightened child does not shout; she whispers. For years I have heard God's daughters whisper one to another of their stirrings within. For almost three decades I have whispered to my husband as we lie in bed. Speaking loudly seems out of place under the cover of night in the warmth of our bed. It is a place of whispers, rest, and intimacy.

There have been times when I have whispered in a worship service as our family sat side by side. I've spoken in hushed tones when I heard something harsh or untrue. "That's not right," I'll whisper. John and my sons nod silently and at times pat my arm in an effort to say, "We understand why you are troubled. You don't need to say it any louder. We hear you."

I whisper as though compelled. It seems wrong to remain silent and not confront what is too small, too exclusive, distorted, or just plain wrong. Perhaps it is the role I hold, but I have to murmur truth in order to snatch away these seeds before they take root. My whisper refutes what is being said out loud.

I whisper when what I hear declared is not what God has whispered to me and underscored in my life. No doubt there are times you have felt the same. If you have heard a God-whisper, then you know it is sacred and worthy of our attention. Often when we teach or preach, we are simply repeating what others have taught us. But when God speaks, it is quite another thing. A God-whisper is no light thing and should be honored.

God is whispering to his sons and daughters. Do you sense this is the time and season to whisper and to listen for the God-whisper? Perhaps you are hearing it even now. Whispers are the dialect of mysteries and foretelling.

For thousands of years the God-whisper was sought, and the search was met far too often with silence.

> There are plenty of prophets and kings who would have given their
> right arm to see what you are seeing but never got so much as a
> glimpse, to hear what you are hearing but never got so much as a
> whisper. (Luke 10:24)

The ancient prophets and kings strained to hear, but God did not so much as murmur. They squinted to grasp the future, but there was nothing to be seen on their horizon. There was no sound, no vision or image, nothing to cause them to ask those in their company, "Did you hear that?"

Then the time came when the message arrived, not in a whisper, but in person. The whispered Word became flesh and spoke out loud as he moved about the people, touching, teaching, healing, and raising the dead. Sadly, the very ones who'd strained to listen, no longer had ears to hear. They missed him because God looked and sounded different from what they'd expected. Jesus whispered to tax collectors and fishermen and yelled at Pharisees.

Rather than explain with his mouth who he was and where he'd come from, Jesus revealed who he was by his life. Through his actions he spoke louder than any words possibly could.

From a Whisper to a Shout

Like many of us, my friend Bobbie Houston listens for the sound of heaven and watches as the Spirit of the Most High frames and forms a mandate for his daughters. She captured what many of us are seeing with these poetic words:

The God-whisper has become a shout.

Women around the world resonate with these words.

More and more of God's daughters are hearing his whisper. What is this God-whisper? And why is the volume increasing? There's a collective outcry for justice that's given rise to a declaration of our hope. When Mary the mother of Jesus received God's promise of salvation for his people, she held it within herself and treasured it in her heart. Today increasing numbers of God's daughters are declaring the life and freedom he is planting in their hearts. As a result, what began as a whisper in individual hearts has become a collective shout. The message is rising above the long containment of quiet.

What I whisper in your ear, shout from the housetops for all to hear!
(Matthew 10:27, NLT)

Jesus first whispered and then told his disciples to shout. He imparted insight and wisdom in private intimacy, then admonished his disciples to openly declare what had been a secret.

I believe we walk the earth in a time period when the God-whispers of yesterday will be elevated to shouts of tomorrow. I am not sure we even understand the possible magnitude of this, but I sense that many of you are even now leaning in and listening. As you draw near, you hear a faint rustling—a stirring within.

The whisper of God is so tantalizing it can frighten.

So provocative it can isolate in its aftermath.

So powerful that, once set into motion, it is impossible to stop.

Thunder crashes and rumbles in the skies.

    Listen! It's God raising his voice!

By his power he stills sea storms,

    by his wisdom he tames sea monsters.

With one breath he clears the sky,

    with one finger he crushes the sea serpent.

And this is only the beginning,

    a mere whisper of his rule.

Whatever would we do if he *really* raised his voice! (Job 26:11–14)

Exactly…what would we do? We certainly would tremble, but those who've known and trusted the whisper would not resist his coming shout. Something deep within us would listen in awe as we waited for his raised voice. All that raw power and the rule of God is merely operating at the whisper level. His exhale clears the sky!

When God first began to whisper life, freedom, hope, strength, wildness, value, and even beauty into my world, it stretched me. He offered me enlargement when there appeared to be no space for me to expand or grow into.

I can best describe my angst this way: Let's say you hear a whisper that there is more to your life than you know, that what you have accepted as all there is to your life was never actually true. The whisper contradicts what you heard declared openly.

Yet the whisper calls to some secret, deep place and awakens a longing yet unexpressed. It rings truer than what you've heard on television or read in books or magazines. With this whispered revelation you are no longer the same. Suddenly you are no longer comfortable in places, relationships, and conversations you were at ease in only a month, week, or day before.

When I first heard God's whisper, this is what happened. On some level I knew I had broken company, but not faith, with what I'd known. I felt as though I had been set adrift, but I had no idea why or how I'd locate my next harbor. All that was stable before now felt unsure, uncertain, and uncomfortable. The only certain thing in my life was that something had shifted, and I would never be the same.

Yes, a whisper has the power to separate us that quickly from what we know—and in just that way. Some might call it an epiphany; others might say it's a paradigm shift.

Whenever I seek out God, he answers in a whisper.

Come close and whisper your answer.
I really need you. (Psalm 55:2)

His answers can cause a degree of separation, and for a season they can be uncomfortable. That's why when we hear a God-whisper, it is crucial that we quiet ourselves, listen, and capture the whisper within.

Ludwig van Beethoven wrote, "Tones sound, and roar and storm about me until I have set them down in notes."[1] What if he had failed to pen the notes he heard within? Not only would we have been robbed of his music; we would have lost the thoughts, love, dreams, and inspirations awakened by his captured symphony of tones.

When God's whisper awakens a storm or roar of thoughts in me, I am restless until I record it. There are many ways to capture a heaven-breathed whisper. Some of us will pen the sound; others will compose it in music. Another may give it voice through messages, drama, or stories that echo its content out loud. Still others may illustrate a creative whisper with art and architecture that lends the whisper form and function.

The method is not important, but recording it is.

LIVE THE WHISPER OUT LOUD

We have all heard the saying, "Live out loud," but I would like to make an addition to this phrase. Live what is within you out loud.

Ralph Waldo Emerson said, "None of us will ever accomplish anything excellent or commanding except when he listens to this whisper which is heard by him alone."[2]

Learn to listen to and for yourself. Don't ask others to tell you what you alone can hear. In doing so, you give them power over the God-whisper within your heart. Honor what God whispers, and take the time to listen to what he imparts in excellence to you.

We are often alone when we hear the whisper. But we are far from the only ones who hear. God is willing to speak to all who are quiet enough to hear. It is just a matter of pausing long enough to hear the Holy Spirit with clarity and then capture his words in strength. Once we have captured our portion of its expression, then we are ready to recognize the whisper in others. Seasons of quiet listening can be uncomfortable, but it is a process we must go through if we are to find ourselves reconnected and steered into a safe harbor.

My season of being alone while listening neared an end in 2006 when I found myself in the Philippines in the company of strong, kind women— Helen, Bobbie, Lisa, and Deborah. We had all traveled from different countries to be part of a launch for a curriculum that brought value and strength to women the world over.

I had no foreknowledge that how I carried myself would be radically altered in this conference. The encounter did not change what I said so much as how I said it. I like to think that at the close of 2006 I had less question and apology in my words.

After the conference I was more intimately connected and truer to God's whisper. Before then I was conflicted, isolated, and very much alone.

As the schedule would have it, I spoke first. When I was finished, I sat and drank in the messages of the other women. Session after session, life poured into my weary, wondering soul. It was as though each woman verbalized my whispers and secrets as they spoke with clarity, strength, anointing, and kindness. I could not stop the tears that traced my cheeks and watered the dry places of my soul. My longings and questions had been answered.

After the last session I rode back to the hotel with a few of them. I stumbled all over myself trying to form words for what was happening within me.

"But these are the very things you write on and speak about," Bobbie commented.

She was right, but until then I had not heard them echoed out loud.

For years I felt as though I'd been alone, speaking words in a confined space. I could see out but couldn't get out until someone suddenly threw open the louvered doors and invited me into a large, open space filled with light and laughter.

Bobbie reached over and patted my leg. "You are not alone anymore."

I nodded and cried, feeling childlike but not caring in the least. That night was a moment and a marker. I am not certain I realized I'd felt alone until that moment when I was included. I was truly one of the sisters who would join the ranks of their brothers and work together to change the world. Being connected with others who had heard this same whisper was empowering, amazing, and freeing.

You may have experienced this too. Have you ever felt like you were on the outside looking in, and all of a sudden you found yourself included? Daughter, sister, mother, and friend, know that you belong. You are not alone. You never were. You are watched for and welcomed by all others who bear God's whisper within.

This inclusion didn't happen because they noticed you weren't invited and felt obligated by good manners. No, not at all. You are included because you belong to a company of women and men who are arising upon the earth.

But you belong. The Holy One anointed you, and you all know it. I haven't been writing this to tell you something you don't know, but to confirm the truth you do know, and to remind you that the truth doesn't breed lies. (1 John 2:20–21)

Discovering I belonged meant the world to me. Even though I traveled and spoke to hundreds of women each week, I often felt like a visitor. Always visiting and never belonging can feel very lonely at times. So let's settle it now, lovely one; you are not a visitor—you are family. When the many are one, words are echoed, relationships are established, and the volume rises. This type of whisper invites us to connect.

So what of the shout?

Don't shout. In fact, don't even speak—not so much as a whisper
until you hear me say, "Shout!"—then shout away! (Joshua 6:10)

There is timing involved when even the thought of a whisper is to be raised to a shout. You see, we walk this earth in a strategic and perilous season. As God did with Jericho, he is going to secretly surround some things and, when the time is right, bring them down with a collective shout.

For the Lord Himself will descend from heaven with a shout, with
the voice of an archangel, and with the trumpet of God. (1 Thessalonians 4:16, NKJV)

At the sound of his voice, the reign of death and destruction will crumble.

The Israelites encircled Jericho seven times before the power to shout was there. Likewise, smart lionesses do not roar unless they are certain of their ambush. This isn't about being loud and raising a shout as much as it is about being strategic. None of us should declare what we are not positioned to carry out in strength.

We should not raise all whispers to the volume of a shout.

Like a woman having a baby,
> writhing in distress, screaming her pain
> as the baby is being born. (Isaiah 26:17)

For years we have individually and corporately screamed our pain, but screaming pain is not the answer. Bringing forth life from the pain of our labor is. Let's redeem the labor, the prejudice, and even the pain in order to give birth to a generation of strong and vibrant daughters.

WHEN THE SHOUT BECOMES A ROAR

Anyone can yell. But not everyone can roar, at least not until it is time.

So what exactly is a roar? A roar is not a super loud shout. It is first and foremost a fearless proclamation. A roar is a release of something primal, uncontainable, and slightly unintelligible. We each have the potential of the roar, but not as individuals. I believe for humans the roar is a collective expression of more than voices. I believe it is the sound of people living their faith out loud while sharing hope and expressing God's love.

Some of you may remember the 1970s Helen Reddy song with the lyrics "I am woman, hear me roar!" Please understand, I am not suggesting that only the women should roar. Nor do I encourage women to roar at men or men to roar at women. I believe it is time we lift our voices and roar together!

Even now I hear in my spirit, "Ready yourselves, daughters, because collectively your shout has the potential to become a roar that will rise upon earth and release the provision from heaven." As Winston Churchill said, "I was not the lion, but it fell to me to give the lion's roar."

Likewise, we are not the lion, but it has fallen to us to give voice to our Lion's roar. Jesus alone is the Christ and the Lion of Judah. We are his followers who echo his roar. What would cause our Lion Lord to roar? I believe answers will be revealed as we explore what causes lions and lionesses in the wild to roar.

Even though both of these big cats roar, the roar of each originates for different reasons. The foremost reason for a lion to roar is to proclaim and protect his territory. As darkness falls, the lead lion (or lions) will rise to his feet, bow his head, expand his chest, and draw in the night air. Then he releases a roar. The sound reverberates throughout his realm to declare, "I am alert, powerful, and present. I'm ready to defend my territory and pride family against all who dare to challenge me. I will not be quiet if anyone attempts to steal my lionesses or cubs. Our food will not be poached by rogues who are not part of our family."

The lion's roar intimidates hyenas. Its power is felt without and within and alerts all that lurk in the shadows that harassment will not be tolerated. The roar terrifies invaders and sets boundaries in place.

Lions also roar to locate the members of their pride. The roar says, "Here I am. Where are you?" The related lionesses and lions answer back with roars of their own.

The strength and volume of the roar reveals a lot of the lion's characteristics. A roar communicates size, age, and physical condition. In essence, his roar says, "I know you don't see me, but do you hear and feel this? Don't mess with me!" Last, but certainly not least, lions roar when they are ticked off.

As I write these words, I cannot help but think of how our Jesus was consumed with a zeal for God's house. Are we likewise impassioned enough to bow our heads, fill our lives, and declare who we are in relationship to him?

Now, what inspires the lioness to roar?

Like the lion, she roars to proclaim and protect her territory and validate her relationship with members of the pride. She will roar to call in the help and protection of other lionesses and ward off enemies. She roars to call in lost or wandering cubs. But the primary reason the lioness roars is to protect her young.

To illustrate this I am borrowing a finding from a two-year study of why lions roar.

> It appears that by banding together, females benefit not only by
> being better able to defend their cubs in direct encounters with
> potentially infanticidal [cub murdering] males, but also because
> by roaring together they minimize the chance that these encounters
> will occur at all.[3]

Lionesses primarily roar together because a lone lioness's roar could be mistaken for an invitation for a nonpride lion to mate with her. The last thing lionesses want to do is to lure in a male who will kill their young and take over their pride. A rogue lion often kills the young so that the lionesses will want to mate with him sooner (lionesses will not mate when they are already raising cubs). This enables him to establish his lineage quicker.

Historically, behaviorists have believed the driving reason behind the lioness's social network was the increased ability to hunt. Now they are questioning the conclusions of the former research and believe that the number one reason lionesses remain in a related group is for the protection of their young, and the secondary reason is for the coordination of their hunting efforts.

When I read that the reason behind the group roar was to prevent the death and destruction of their children, I almost wept. In the study they learned that a group of just three lionesses who roared together was enough to deter infanticide.[4]

What does this say to us?

By yourself you're unprotected.
With a friend you can face the worst.
Can you round up a third?
A three-stranded rope isn't easily snapped. (Ecclesiastes 4:12)

If lionesses know their young are not safe when they are isolated from other lionesses, why do we try to be so independent? Together we can protect the young from death and destruction. Isolated we don't have a chance.

> Never believe that a few caring people can't change the world. For, indeed, that's all who ever have.
>
> —MARGARET MEAD

This being the case, why are we so frightened to admit our need for each other? We don't have to engage the masses; we just need a few caring, compassionate people to change the world for the masses.

PRAYER ROARS

Only related lionesses dare to roar unafraid. They know they need not only the voice but also the protection of the sisters.

So why should we, the lioness daughters of God, roar?

We lift our voice to declare his powerful domain and our allegiance. We roar to call in the lost. Our sound will guide the young and wandering safely home. We shake the air to check the movements of trespassers, enemies, and thieves. Together we raise the roar to protect our young from death and destruction. We will not face the darkness in silence.

I can't imagine any better reason than those above. Even now I'm angry that we've been silent for so long. We had no right to be silent when we've been charged to speak up for those who have no voice. The hour is late. Darkness grew unchecked while we slept. Now that we are awake, we must pray that God will multiply our efforts as we magnify his light. Prayer is our most powerful reason for gathering. We will need heaven's protection, wisdom, and strategies to wage this war.

Jesus said, "Love the Lord your God with all your passion and prayer and intelligence" (Matthew 22:37).

Here are three instrumental ways we can lift the volume to the level of a roar with our passion, prayers, and intelligence. As we consecrate these three areas of our lives, they merge until we love God with passionate, intelligent prayers.

We start small and believe big. God promises to be present whenever two or more gather in his name. Prayer paves the way for provision, purpose, and strategies. Lioness sister, I bet you could find two women to pray alongside you…even if it's by phone.

As we rise, gather, and lift our voices, may God cause groups of three to multiply quickly into groups of thirty. Then may the thirty sisters increase tenfold and become three hundred. The three hundred multiplies into three thousand, then thirty thousand, and so on until we are an army whose prayers ascend from earth to heaven as a mighty roar. It is high time we echo our Lion's roar.

Rise like Lions after slumber
In unvanquishable number,
Shake your chains to earth like dew
Which in sleep had fallen on you—
Ye are many—they are few.
  —Percy Bysshe Shelley[5]

Lioness, lift your voice.

Discussion Questions

1. When you ponder the imagery of the lioness, what would you like to learn? *(Chapter 1)*

2. The dynamic of "stretch" happens when tension, flex, or strain is added. An ability to stretch can produce increased flexibility and prevent injury. What are some of the areas in your life that need to be stretched? What are some areas that have already been stretched? How does the lioness initially stretch your perception of yourself? *(Chapter 2)*

3. What does the concept "at ease with strength and at rest with power" impress upon you? *(Chapter 2)*

4. "Then our lioness sighs contently as she sums up her beauty: 'I am fearfully and wonderfully made.'" Is it easy for you to see yourself as fearfully and wonderfully made? Why or why not? *(Chapter 4)*

5. Those of us who are strong and able in the faith need to step in and lend a hand to those who falter, and not just do what is most convenient for us. Strength is for service, not status. Each one of us needs to look after the good of the people around us, asking ourselves "How can I help?" (Rom. 15:1–2, MSG). What is currently an area of strength in your life that you could use to help others? *(Chapter 5)*

6. "Gender alone does not qualify a man to lead, just as gender alone should not disqualify a woman. Virtue qualifies both male and female." What is your reaction to this statement? Why do you take that position? *(Chapter 6)*

7. *"So clean the inside by giving gifts to the poor, and you will be clean all over"* (Luke 11:41, NLT). Generosity to those who cannot return your kindness is the ultimate internal cleanse. To whom can you give gifts of time, money, or service in order to see this type of clean up happen? *(Chapter 7)*

8. *Prowess* is defined as: exceptional ability, skill, or strength; exceptional valor or bravery. If you have prowess you might say, "I don't know or do everything, but what I know, I choose to do well." What ability, skill, or strength is waiting for you to make it exceptional? *(Chapter 8)*

9. Do you believe every child deserves an equal chance to survive? If so, how has this translated to how you respond to your neighbors or the children in your immediate world? *(Chapter 8)*

10. "Are you tired? Worn out? Burned out on religion? Come to me. Get away with me and you'll recover your life. I'll show you how to take a real rest. Walk with me and work with me—watch how I do it. Learn the unforced rhythms of grace. I won't lay anything heavy or ill-fitting on you. Keep company with me and you'll learn to live freely and lightly"(Matt. 11:28–30, MSG). Is there an area of life that is presently weighing on you? Is this an area in which you are not "keeping company" with Jesus? *(Chapter 9)*

11. We need to look ahead, realizing that our present choices live on. What hard choices are you making today so that others beyond your time will live well? *(Chapter 9)*

12. Jesus said to His disciples: "'Anyone who intends to come with me has to let me lead. You're not in the driver's seat; I am. Don't run from suffering; embrace it. Follow me and I'll show you how. Self-help is no help at all. Self-sacrifice is the way, my way, to finding yourself, your true self'" (Matt. 16:24–25, MSG). Where is God leading you to that you are afraid to follow Him? *(Chapter 10)*

13. Who in your world is a present-day legendary lioness? What will she be remembered for long after she's gone? What do you want to be remembered for? *(Chapter 10)*

14. What areas of life have been made uncomfortable for you because God has whispered life, freedom, wildness, beauty, and value into them? *(Chapter 11)*

15. Timing is crucial; we live in strategic and perilous times. God is secretly surrounding some things; and when the time is right, He will bring them down with a shout! What areas is God asking you to surround with prayer? *(Chapter 11)*

List of Organizations

Pearl Alliance

www.pearlalliance.org

Pearl Alliance, an outreach of Messenger International, raises funds and awareness to combat human trafficking and rescue those who are already enslaved. Their current area of focus is Cambodia and Thailand.

The Colour Sisterhood

www.thecoloursisterhood.com

Hillsong Church

The Colour Sisterhood represents a company of down-to-earth, everyday women who desire to make a difference and make the world a better place. In essence, it is a foundation seeking to place value upon humanity; a story of unity and alliance.

Life Outreach International—*RESCUE*LIFE

www.lifetoday.org

James and Betty Robison

*RESCUE*LIFE is helping to reach, rescue, and restore children in three of the largest global human-trafficking markets: India, Cambodia, and Thailand.

The A21 Campaign

www.TheA21Campaign.org

The A21 Campaign aims to fight human trafficking by raising awareness, taking legal action where appropriate, and offering rehabilitation services to rescued victims of human trafficking in order to fight this injustice from a comprehensive approach. Their current area of focus is Eastern Europe.

Notes

Chapter 2: A Force Unseen

1. Nicholas D. Kristof and Sheryl WuDunn, *Half the Sky: Turning Oppression into Opportunity for Women Worldwide* (New York: Knopf, 2009), xx.
2. Kristof and WuDunn, *Half the Sky,* xx.
3. Kristof and WuDunn, *Half the Sky,* xxi.
4. Kristof and WuDunn, *Half the Sky,* 250.

Chapter 3: Dangerously Awake

1. Nicholas D. Kristof and Sheryl WuDunn, *Half the Sky: Turning Oppression into Opportunity for Women Worldwide* (New York: Knopf, 2009), xviii.

Chapter 6: Under the Same Mission

1. Lisa Bevere, *Fight Like a Girl: The Power of Being a Woman* (New York: Warner Faith, 2006), 42.
2. Sue Monk Kidd, *The Dance of the Dissident Daughter: A Woman's Journey from Christian Tradition to the Sacred Feminine* (New York: HarperCollins, 1996), 27.
3. Marianne Williamson, *A Woman's Worth* (New York: Random House, 1993), 20.
4. Williamson, *A Woman's Worth,* 21.
5. Williamson, *A Woman's Worth,* 21.
6. "What's Your Quotation Quotient?" *Monterey County Herald,* May 4, 2010, www.montereyherald.com/entertainment/ci_14961372.

Chapter 8: Lionesses Are Strategic

1. *Random House Webster's College Dictionary,* s.v. "prowess."
2. Margaret Mead, ThinkExist.com, http://thinkexist.com/quotation/sister_is_probably_the_most_competitive/12512.html.
3. Lisa Bevere, *Nurture: Give and Get What You Need to Flourish* (New York: Hachette, 2008), 57.

Chapter 10: Walking with a Lion

1. C. S. Lewis, *Prince Caspian: The Return to Narnia* (New York: Harper-Collins, 1979), 131–32.
2. Lewis, *Prince Caspian,* 149.
3. Lewis, *Prince Caspian,* 150.
4. Alan Axelrod, *Elizabeth I, CEO: Strategic Lessons from the Leader Who Built an Empire* (Paramus, NJ: Prentice Hall, 2000), 6.
5. Axelrod, *Elizabeth I, CEO,* 250.
6. Axelrod, *Elizabeth I, CEO,* 83–85.

Chapter 11: From a Whisper to a Roar

1. Ludwig van Beethoven, ThinkExist.com, http://thinkexist.com/quotes/ludwig_van_beethoven/2.html.
2. Ralph Waldo Emerson, ThinkExist.com, http://thinkexist.com/quotation/none_of_us_will_ever_accomplish_anything/223531.html.
3. Jon Grinnell, "The Lion's Roar: More Than Just Hot Air," *Zoogoer,* May–June 1997, http://nationalzoo.si.edu/Publications/ZooGoer/1997/3/lionsroar.cfm.
4. Grinnell, "The Lion's Roar."
5. Percy Bysshe Shelley, *The Mask of Anarchy,* Art of Europe, www.artofeurope.com/shelley/she5.htm.

united states
PO BOX 888
PALMER LAKE, CO 80133-0888

T: 800.648.1477 *us and canada
T: 719.487.3000

mail@MessengerInternational.org

For more information
please contact us:

Messenger International.
life-transforming truth.

europe
PO BOX 1066
HEMEL, HEMPSTEAD
HP2 7GQ
UNITED KINGDOM

T: 0800 9808 933
(OUTSIDE UK)
T: +44 1442 288 531

europe@MessengerInternational.org

SIGN UP
to receive e-mails from John & Lisa Bevere
Visit us online at
www.MessengerInternational.org

australia
ROUSE HILL TOWN CENTRE
PO BOX 6444
ROUSE HILL NSW 2155

T: 1.300.650.577
(OUTSIDE AUS)
T: +61 2 9679 4900

aus@MessengerInternational.org

 Follow John & Lisa Bevere on **facebook**. & **twitter**
for updates & information on meetings.

Books by Lisa

Be Angry, But Don't Blow It!
Fight Like a Girl
Kissed the Girls and Made Them Cry
Lioness Arising
Nurture
Out of Control and Loving It!
The True Measure of a Woman
You Are Not What You Weigh

Awaken.
You too are a lioness.

In *Lioness Arising*, author and speaker Lisa Bevere offers the life and image of the lioness as a fierce and tender model for women. Revealing the surprising characteristics of this amazing creature, Lisa challenges women to discover fresh passion, prowess, and purpose.

Learn what it means to:
- be a stunning representation of strength
- fiercely protect the young
- lend your voice to the silenced
- live in the light and hunt in the dark
- raise a collective roar that changes everything

Packed with remarkable insights from nature and a rich depth of biblical references to lionesses, *Lioness Arising* is a call for women to rise up in strength and numbers to change their world.

Curriculum Includes:
- 8 Video Sessions on 3 DVDs (30 minutes each)
- 8 Audio Sessions on 4 CDs (30 minutes each)
- *Lioness Arising* Hardcover Book
- Safari Guide
- Promotional Materials to help gather groups

Order Today! www.MessengerInternational.org

Together—we are His lioness arising.

TOGETHER WE CAN MAKE A DIFFERENCE

The women and children who are exploited by human trafficking are precious treasures lost in darkness. They must be heard and recovered. Pearl Alliance raises funds and awareness to prevent the progression of human trafficking and rescue those already enslaved.

Join Us! www.PearlAlliance.org | www.twitter.com/pearlalliance